MUSEUMS DISCOVERED

The Wadsworth Atheneum

We gratefully acknowledge the staff of the Wadsworth Atheneum,
especially Gregory Hedberg, Cecil B. Adams, Anne Buckley, and
William N. Hosley, Jr., for their participation, and thank Marguerite O'Brien
for her assistance in the production of this book.

Edited by Wendy Shore

Editorial staff: Eve Sinaiko,
Sandra Moy, and Anthony Strianse

Color photography by Gordon H. Roberton;
pages 33, 54, 96, 117, 151, and 193 photographed
by Joseph Szaszfai; page 69 by E. Irving Blomstrann;
photograph of A. Everett Austin on page 9 by Deford Dechert.

ISBN: O-9605574-3-1
Library of Congress Card Catalog Number: 81-85340

Created for Penshurst Books by
Shorewood Fine Art Books, Inc.
475 Tenth Avenue
New York, N.Y. 10018

MUSEUMS DISCOVERED

The Wadsworth Atheneum

by Gerald Silk

with twenty essays contributed by Alison de Lima Greene

Penshurst Books
Ft. Lauderdale, Florida

Created by Shorewood Fine Art Books, New York

Introduction

On July 31, 1844, the Wadsworth Atheneum in Hartford, Connecticut, opened its doors, and any visitor paying twenty-five cents could enter and view a collection of art that the local newspaper, the *Hartford Courant*, described as "an attraction probably unsurpassed by any in the country." Housing eighty-two objects, mostly paintings, and rich in the modern American art of the time, the Atheneum, whose history is studded with "firsts," began as a pioneer. It was America's first civic, publically incorporated art museum and although it shared a building with a Young Men's Institute (which later became the Hartford Public Library) and the Connecticut Historical Society, its gallery space was preeminent and distinct. Here, art exclusively was displayed, though in most museums of the day fossils, skeletons, and other natural and scientific curiosities—often the major draws—were liberally interspersed with traditional works of fine art. The Atheneum, today one of the country's major museums, remains America's oldest continuously operating public museum, and its collection, numbering in the vicinity of 40,000 objects, spanning 3,000 years of art history, and embracing all the major fine, applied, and decorative arts, resides in a five-building complex. The facade of the original structure still stands and the previous jumble and clash of several discrete architectural styles have been harmonized and made more coherent through a recent building program; thus the architecture of the Atheneum, in its tradition, diversity, and progress, exemplifies the history of the museum itself.

The early history of the Wadsworth Atheneum is much the story of its namesake and founder, Daniel Wadsworth. Wadsworth, a well-to-do Hartford philanthropist, was something of a dilettante. His pursuits included architecture and furniture reproduction and he was a patron and collector of the fine arts, particularly of American painting of the first half of the nineteenth century. His wealth derived mainly from his father, Jeremiah Wadsworth, who had become wealthy while being a patriot. The elder Wadsworth served as commissary to the revolutionary forces both in Connecticut and France, and amassed the capital upon which he built his fortune by marketing French goods in the United States.

Daniel Wadsworth's interest in the arts began early when, at the age of twelve, he accompanied his father to Europe. There the youth visited museums, libraries, and studios, and sat for a portrait with his father, painted by John Trumbull. Trumbull, soon to become one of America's foremost artists, was the son of Jonathan Trumbull, the Governor of Connecticut and a friend of Jeremiah Wadsworth. The Wadsworth-Trumbull nexus, cemented with Daniel's marriage to the painter's niece Faith in 1791, is essential to the history of the Atheneum. Trumbull advised Wadsworth on the practice and purchase of art, and introduced him to the American landscape painter Thomas Cole; Wadsworth fast became Cole's friend and sponsor. It is no surprise, therefore, that the main holdings and attractions in the Atheneum's early collection were works by Cole and

"Portrait of Jeremiah Wadsworth and His Son
Daniel Wadsworth," *by John Trumbull*

Trumbull.

In his twenties, Wadsworth began making landscape sketches and in his thirties developed an interest in architecture. As a painter of landscape, he felt an affinity with the emerging group of American artists who also loved this subject, many of whom would soon become known as the Hudson River School. Landscape, capable of inspiring the spiritual, the sublime, and the magnificent in an increasingly Romantic, yet optimistic age, and at the same time able to evoke the distinctively native in a country sorely lacking in tradition, became America's most outstanding theme in art in the mid-1820s. Thus Wadsworth was to befriend, patronize, advise, and occasionally influence painters such as Cole and Frederick Edwin Church, and this involvement is reflected today in the strength of the Atheneum's nineteenth-century American landscape collection.

If Wadsworth's interest in landscape painting is linked to Romanticism, then his tastes in architecture suggest a similar sentiment. Sometime between 1805–09, he designed and built an impressive residence on Talcott Mountain in Avon, Connecticut, about five miles from Hartford. Significantly, this house is one of the first examples of Gothic Revival architecture in America, which was also to be the style of the Wadsworth Atheneum. This villa, called Monte Video, and its surrounding territory also became the subject of paintings by Trumbull and Cole (Cole's *View of Monte Video, the Seat of Daniel Wadsworth, Esq.* of 1828 belongs to the Atheneum).

Wadsworth's devotion to art culminated in his project for the establishment of Hartford's own art museum. This idea grew out of discussions with Trumbull, who was concerned about the fate of his own art and collection. The initial plan to divide Trumbull's holdings between separate galleries located in New Haven and Hartford never materialized and instead Yale University received Trumbull's collection, installing it in its art gallery, which opened in 1832. Wadsworth, however, still envisioned a major art museum for Hartford, and when the city's only exhibition space—the Hartford Gallery of Art—closed in 1841, he set his plan in motion. Following a tradition established in Boston, Wadsworth proposed the creation of an atheneum, a kind of cultural center, in which a library, a historical society, and an art gallery would be housed together. Named after the Greek goddess of wisdom, art, and culture, these atheneums were intended, in a somewhat benign, exclusive, and gentlemanly way, to be modern-day centers of learning, patterned after what were thought to have been ancient meeting places where scholars, students, and intellectuals gathered and exchanged ideas. Often more clubbish than scholarly, these societies generally devoted more space to smoking rooms filled with comfortable armchairs than to display space for the exhibition of art. Wadsworth, however, was a renegade: art was the focal point rather than the periphery of his Atheneum.

In 1841, in conjunction with several other leading Hartford citizens, Wadsworth devised a charter "for the establishment of a gallery of fine art," and began raising money for the construction of the Atheneum. He also donated the land occupied by his father's Main Street homestead as the site for the museum and moved the house to another location. Though there is some speculation that the initial

The Wadsworth Atheneum circa 1900

architectural plans for the building were drawn up by Wadsworth in consultation with Henry Barnard, the architects of record are unquestionably Ithiel Town and Alexander J. Davis, leading advocates of the Gothic Revival style that Wadsworth so admired. Groundbreaking took place in 1842, and the structure was finished in 1844. It was built of cream-colored South Glastonbury granite and was two stories high, with towers attached to each corner, and taller turrets embracing the central zone, which contained a large portal and a magnificent arched window. Its Gothic style summoned up a sense of the Romantic, though to some it recalled religious architecture and thus suggested the common association of museums with sanctuaries and of works of art with sacred objects.

As was common in the establishment of public institutions, the construction of the Atheneum did not always proceed smoothly. It was plagued by cost overruns and when the building was completed there was no money in the initial fund to stock the museum with art. An ingenious solution was the decision to "rent" much of the art at the cost of the interest on the principal, with the intention to purchase it when funds became available. Fortunately for the Atheneum, a substantial number of works was available from the recently defunct American Academy of Fine Arts in New York. The true gems of this collection included John Vanderlyn's controversial *Death of Jane McCrea* (page 143), Rembrandt Peale's candlelight *Self-Portrait* (page 147), and what was to be the most popular piece of the museum's early years, Sir Thomas Lawrence's full-length portrait of Benjamin West. The collection was rounded out by the purchase of a group of Trumbulls, including five half-size copies from his famous series of revolutionary and battle scenes; a Cole landscape; and the obligatory copy of Gilbert Stuart's full-length *George Washington*, painted this time by James Ellsworth. Upon Wadsworth's death in 1848, the museum was bequeathed many of his holdings, including six more Trumbulls and five more Coles, considerably enhancing the already solid American collection. In this early formation of the collection, European art, though not scant, was considerably weaker; many works were copies, of dubious authenticity, or by minor artists.

The launching of this institution in a town with fewer than 10,000 inhabitants was remarkable, and its strong representation of what would have been considered "Modern American Art" was both striking and bold. The next half-century of activity at the Atheneum, however, was less radical. The museum acquired its first semi-official curator in 1845 with the appointment of Edward Sheffield Bartholomew. Bartholomew, a sculptor himself, departed for Italy in 1850 and upon his death in 1858 the contents of his studio were bought with funds raised by the museum. From the 1850s to the late 1880s, the museum lapsed into complacency and there were few significant additions to the collection or the physical plant. But in the late eighties, a flurry of activity began that has grown and has continued almost unabated up to the present.

The major stimulus for action and development came from Reverend Francis Goodwin, who, after he became President of the Board of Trustees around 1890, initiated "a plan of re-organization" for the museum. Goodwin was well connected, and half the funds he raised for this project came from his cousins in the Morgan family. Improvements to the building started in 1893 with the complete reconstruction of the Atheneum's interior and the addition of a wing to house the Watkinson Library. The collection was augmented with gifts and purchases of works from the collections of Batterson and of Samuel Beresford,

acquired partly through monies provided by the Henry and Walter Keney Fund. What is noteworthy about these acquisitions is their inclusion of European works of good quality, especially in the area of Northern Renaissance and Northern Baroque painting.

The tempo of growth picked up enormously in the first decades of the twentieth century. Two new buildings were constructed: one was donated in 1905 by Elizabeth Hart Jarvis Colt and erected in 1906–07, in memory of her husband, Samuel Colt, a Hartford resident and the inventor of the revolver. Designed and constructed by Benjamin Wistar Morriss of New York, the Colt Memorial was a small English Tudor structure, created to house the Colt bequest of firearms, decorative arts, and paintings. The other major addition was the mammoth Morgan building, also done by Morriss in a Renaissance Revival style. Built between 1908 and 1910, it was enlarged in 1916. This space was given by J. Pierpont Morgan, Sr. in memory of his father, Junius Spencer Morgan, financier and Hartford citizen. The Morgan Memorial, as imposing as the Colt wing was modest, personified the powerful and sometimes rapacious collecting habits of the Morgans; the two structures, along with the original Wadsworth edifice, demonstrated how the desire of individual benefactors to leave their distinct imprints on the museum created a diverse, often discordant array of facades and interior spaces.

Impressive as these new structures were, the Wadsworth Atheneum again possessed important physical facilities without enough art to put in them. This time, the Morgan family came to the rescue. In 1917, J. Pierpont Morgan, Jr. gave a portion of the collection of his father, who had died in 1913, to the Atheneum. Although many spectacular items in the collection went to the Metropolitan Museum in New York City, the material received by the Wadsworth was still of such high quality that this one magnanimous gesture instantly elevated the Hartford institution from a pleasant and interesting gallery to a major museum of international repute.

The main categories of the Morgan bequest included a superb group of French and German porcelains, seventeenth-century gilt objects, paintings from the Italian Renaissance, and uniquely valuable Greek, Roman, and Early Christian bronzes. The bronzes and porcelains were the most outstanding contributions, the latter containing the largest collection of Meissen figurines outside of Europe.

Morgan beneficence also brought to the museum the Wallace Nutting Collection of American Furniture in 1926. Nutting, a minister and photographer, as well as a scholar and author of several books on furniture, developed a comprehensive assemblage of objects from what he called the "Pilgrim Century" (1620–1720). In order to repurchase his furniture reproduction factory, which he believed was ruining his reputation through the manufacture of poor-quality copies, Nutting sold his collection to Morgan in the 1920s. Morgan then presented the works to the Atheneum.

As these various gifts suggest, the Wadsworth was making tremendous progress in the area of the decorative arts; meanwhile, advances in acquisitions of paintings lagged. This deficiency, however, was corrected with a vengeance beginning in the late 1920s. The coincidence of two key events characterizes this next episode in the Atheneum's history. First was the establishment of the Sumner Fund to create The Ella Gallup Sumner and Mary Catlin Sumner Collection; second was the appointment of A. Everett Austin, Jr. as director of the museum. The bequest from the estate of Frank C. Sumner, made in memory of his sister-in-law and wife to purchase "choice paintings," came at an economically propitious moment and provided the means with which the dashing Austin, a Harvard-trained connoisseur and amateur actor and magician, embarked on a buying spree that brought a first-rank and often riveting series of works to the Wadsworth Atheneum. Although his first purchases, a work from the school of Fra Angelico, a Daumier, and a Tintoretto, demonstrated that his tastes ranged from the delicate through the dramatic to the dynamic, Austin shaped a collection that reflected his own love of the theatrical, and thus Baroque art was his main passion.

Austin's selection of Baroque paintings was acute, for he bought works of this style at low prices well before they were thought of as highly prized commodities in the art world. The proudest possession was obtained somewhat late in Austin's tenure—Caravaggio's *Ecstasy of St. Francis* (page 27). An exquisite work in its own right and one of the rare works by Caravaggio in America, *Ecstasy of St. Francis* was also pivotal to the museum's extensive and often stunning Baroque holdings. It was Caravaggio who frequently pioneered and perfected such techniques as dramatic chiaroscuro, diagonally arranged composition, and dynamic, emotional action—characteristics that became the foundation of the Baroque style. The followers of Caravaggio, both

A. Everett Austin, Jr., director of the museum, in 1941, as Hamlet

direct and indirect, were widespread and legion, and the breadth of the Atheneum's Baroque collection attests to his legacy: Italian acolytes are well represented with paintings by Orazio Gentileschi and Carlo Saraceni; Spanish with Zurbarán and Jusepe de Ribera; French with Nicolas Poussin and Simon Vouet; and Northern European with Peter Paul Rubens and Anthony van Dyck. Some of these Baroque acquisitions were made after Austin's departure; nevertheless, he set the tone for the purchase of prime works from the period, and the generous Sumner Fund continues to allow the museum to buy with a similar acumen and zeal.

The Austin era was the heyday of the Atheneum. Its whirlwind pace was notably boosted with the construction of a new building in 1934. The museum decided in 1932 to use the monies accumulated in a building fund established in 1918 by Samuel Putnam Avery, who had also donated many works. Just as Daniel Wadsworth relinquished the site of his father's house for the original museum building, now

The Avery Court of the museum

Daniel's own home was sacrificed to the cause of museum expansion (although in this instance, the residence was demolished rather than relocated). On this parcel of land, the Avery Memorial was built by the New York firm of Morris and O'Connor. In an attempt to keep the styles of the various facades from clashing, the architects created a subtle Art Deco front, intended to blend with the abutting Morgan Memorial. While the exterior of Avery appears conservative, the interior is radical and daring. It is, perhaps, the first example in the United States of the modern International Style, which soon became popular in American museum architecture. In addition to containing the most modern display space for fine art in the country, the Avery Wing, reflecting Austin's thespian bent, housed the first theater of any museum in the States, in which a highly ambitious series of plays, dance, film, music, and lectures was scheduled. In this respect, the Wadsworth Atheneum brought the American museum world into the twentieth century; it was the pioneer in conceiving the function of such institutions to be comprehensive.

Avery Memorial opened with a flourish. Its inaugural exhibition was a major Picasso restrospective, the first of its kind in the world. Premiering in the theater was the extraordinary Gertrude Stein-Virgil Thomson opera *Four Saints in Three Acts*. The staging of such a work, with its delightfully disarming sets and costumes, designed by Florine Stettheimer, was a bold, avant-garde event that attracted luminaries and socialites from all over the country. The train from New York to Hartford was packed with first-nighters and the opening was an *affaire célèbre*. In a similar spirit,

Austin arranged for the debut performance of George Balanchine's ballet company at the Avery theater. The aforementioned Picasso exhibition, exceptional as it was, was only one of several major shows launched by Austin. From 1928 to 1945, the director packed the calendar with exhibits as varied as *Italian Painting of the Sei- and Settecento* (1930), *Newer Super Realism* (1931), *Literature and Poetry in Painting since 1850* (1933), *Abstract Art—Gabo, Pevsner, Mondrian, Domela* (1935), *Georges de la Tour and the Brothers Le Nain* (1936), *The John Wise Collection of Ancient Peruvian Art* (1937), and *Men in Arms* (1943). Moreover, in the spirit of the museum's originator, Austin avidly collected contemporary art, acquiring works by Picasso, Mondrian, Cornell, Dali, Miró, Demuth, Hopper, Ernst and de Chirico, to mention but a few. Many of these were displayed in the Avery Court, the most striking space of the new wing. In a brilliant piece of installation, the clean and sleek court has as its centerpiece a sixteenth-century Mannerist sculpture by Pietro Francavilla, in which a languid and attenuated Venus is intertwined with both a satyr, grinning impishly, and a nymph with a glazed, almost erotic expression. Here, once again, past meets present at the Atheneum, but in this instance the encounter proves provocative rather than disconcerting.

A further Austin accomplishment worth noting was his procurement of the Serge Lifar Collection of ballet set and costume design. Lifar, a principal of Diaghilev's corps, was bequeathed the master's collection of dance-related objects and designs in 1929. It consists mostly of works for the Ballet Russe and incorporates designs by a stellar group of artists including Picasso, Braque, Matisse, Bakst, Benois, Gris, Derain, Miró, Léger, Gabo, de Chirico, and Rouault. Obtained by the museum through the Sumner Fund in 1933, the Lifar Collection, compatible with Austin's love of the performing arts, must also have seemed a fitting prelude to the museum's innovative presentation, just a year later, of dances by Balanchine, who was Diaghilev's last ballet master.

With Austin's departure in 1945, Charles C. Cunningham succeeded to the directorship of the museum. He assumed power during the war years, when cultural activity was severely curtailed. Properly, Cunningham, a traditional art historian, while continuing to respect the direction and rhythm established by Austin, set his own course and pace, and this period is marked by numerous distinguished acquisitions. With the Sumner Fund still healthy, Cunningham enriched the already superlative Baroque collection through both purchases and gifts, adding, in particular, important works from Northern Europe by Hals, Rubens, Van Dyck, Ruisdael, and Van Goyen. American art, both modern and older, also received special attention, and pieces by Homer, Eakins, Durand, Gifford, Heade, Inness, Sloan, Henri, Prendergast, Hopper, Shahn, Davis, and Wyeth entered the collection. Of particular significance was the munificence of Henry Schnakenberg, who both donated art and established a fund in 1951 to buy the work of living American artists. In addition, during Cunningham's directorship, the Hartford Public Library and the Connecticut Historical Society moved out of the Atheneum complex and relocated in separate quarters: art, and art alone, was now sufficient in constituting Hartford's major cultural center.

In an evocation of the energetic Austin era, the next director, James Elliott, who served from 1966 to 1976, encouraged a resurgence of activity at the Atheneum. During his tenure, the Education Department was greatly expanded, the docent program (the training of volunteer guides) was instituted, and active relationships with local minority groups and local artists were encouraged, along with a general diversification of programming and an emphasis on contemporary art. The most outstanding development during the Elliott years was the completion of a major architectural program in 1969, which had been initiated in 1962 under Cunningham. The linchpin of this project was the James L. Goodwin building, which was erected on the site of the old Watkinson Library, and it provided the final link in a chain of buildings which, in effect, made the Atheneum a closed "circle" of structures surrounding the open E. Clayton Gengras Court, where outdoor sculpture was placed. In addition, the interiors of the Wadsworth and Colt buildings were gutted and reconstructed, with the intention of unifying what had been an architectural potpourri.

Essential as the building program was, it almost proved the undoing of the Atheneum, and Elliott's many plans had to be curtailed. Reminiscent of the financial woes associated with Daniel Wadsworth's original Gothic Revival structure, the Goodwin building and its attendant alterations cost far more than originally anticipated. Like so many ambitious and well-meaning projects of the 1960s in government, universities, cities, and the cultural world, the Goodwin building in particular and the Wadsworth Atheneum in general became victims of a belief in unlimited economic growth. Furthermore, the Atheneum, like many such institutions, had little experience with seeking funding from sources other than a small coterie of private individuals. To enlist aid from major corporations may have seemed counter to the spirit of an exclusive institution, but by the late 1960s this was the way to maintain fiscal well-being. Thus, by the mid-1970s, the Atheneum was in dire financial straits.

Enter Tracy Atkinson in 1977 as the museum's new and current director, who was obliged to carry out a series of drastic cutbacks in staff and services, already implemented in part before his arrival. Atkinson, an excellent administrator as well as an art historian, was precisely what the Wadsworth needed. Efforts were launched to attract both corporate support and private funding and to increase museum membership. These efforts required that the Atheneum alter its image, and among other things a clever advertising campaign was initiated in hopes of making the museum appear more accessible and less forbidding. The voracious acquisitiveness that had characterized the Atheneum since the Austin days was of necessity slowed. Atkinson felt that the collection was basically solid. As a result, acquisition of art ranked low on his scale of priorities. His major concern, aside from guaranteeing the fiscal stability of the museum, became the careful and deliberate refurbishing and modernization of the physical plant, so that the many museum possessions could be properly displayed, catalogued, conserved, stored, and safeguarded. Atkinson also began addressing a problem that was the reverse of a former situation at the Atheneum: in the past, there had often not been enough art to cover the walls and fill the display cases; now, nearly eighty-five percent of the collection languishes out of sight of the viewing public in storage areas. Atkinson's present "Project Iceberg" is designed to elevate this submerged material to the level of the museum, where the public can properly appreciate it.

It is something of a paradox that while retrenchment and cost-cutting personify the spirit of many museums in the 1970s, blockbuster shows have also become a feature of this period. This is due, in part, to the shift in patronage away from individuals and toward corporations, which generally desire to sponsor exhibitions of major proportion and stature. Moreover, in an age when museums, despite the aid of industry, are constantly in financial need, justification for their support may best be indicated through the popularity of their programs, and blockbuster shows tend to attract more people.

Atkinson, while not averse to the occasional "big show," and devoutly committed to boosting museum attendance, endorses the more frugal approach of exploiting the Wadsworth's own holdings and mounting relatively modest exhibitions. He has built upon a precedent established by ex-director James Elliott for just this kind of program. In 1975, Elliott inaugurated MATRIX, a changing exhibition of contemporary art in a small space off Avery Court, with monies provided by the National Endowment for the Arts. Reflecting the plurality and diversity of modern developments in art, MATRIX has included one-person exhibitions of video performance, architecture, environment, and photography, as well as painting and sculpture, site-specific installations, and an exciting series of public lectures. While one out of three shows has signalled a U.S. museum debut for the artist, well-known figures such as Andy Warhol, Andrew Wyeth, Ed Ruscha, Malcolm Morely, and Eva Hesse have also participated. On a parsimonious budget, MATRIX has managed to present over sixty-five exhibitions in its first six years, keeping Atheneum visitors exceptionally well informed about the art of their time.

The value of MATRIX extends beyond its tantalizing calendar of events. In addition to serving as the stimulus for the development of similar programs at other museums throughout this country, proving the appeal of small exhibitions in continuous series, MATRIX has spawned related projects at the Atheneum. These include *In Focus*, in which historical problems are investigated, based upon works in the collection. Among the more noteworthy recent *In Focus* events have been shows on Daniel Wadsworth, Gerrit Rietveld, and Le Corbusier. The next offspring of MATRIX will be *Dossier*. Reminiscent of the Viking "Art in Context" series of books, *Dossier* will select a single work for in-depth exploration, placing it in a full social and historical context.

Like most major museums, the Wadsworth Atheneum also has a lively community-oriented program. One of the most significant activities is the *Lion's Gallery of the Senses*, a space that engages all of the senses of the individual in the understanding of art. Founded in 1972 with the support of district Lion's Clubs, the gallery's intended purpose was to make art more accessible to the handicapped and the blind, but it has since become a favorite room for all

An interior of the museum

museum-goers, especially children.

As the history of the Wadsworth Atheneum suggests, this venerable institution has always demonstrated great energy and resilience. Despite its recent economic troubles, the Atheneum remains robust, principally because years of perspicacious collecting have given it the lifeblood of any museum—great works of art. Encompassing the entire history of Western art, the collection is strongest in the areas of Baroque art, nineteenth-century American painting, French and German porcelains, and early American furniture. Mindful of the past, as it is the nature of a museum to be, the Atheneum has never neglected the present. As of this writing, the museum, in its frequent role as innovator, has just installed a massive work by a Hartford native and one of the most contemporary of American artists, Sol LeWitt, and this acquisition is particularly bold because the piece is drawn directly on one of the museum walls. Yet, as the visitor walks through the galleries, he is also likely to encounter the oldest extant American portrait (also executed by a New England artist), and though this portrait of Elizabeth Eggington and the wall piece by LeWitt may seem worlds apart, it is precisely this kind of visual juxtaposition that makes the museum so invigorating a place. For close to a century and a half, the illuminating display of artifacts from the cultures of the past and present has kept the Wadsworth Atheneum a vital institution.

Plate List

The European Collection

GREEK

Draped Warrior

Late sixth century B.C.
Bronze
13.5 cm. high (5 5/16 in.)
Gift of J. Pierpont Morgan
Acquisition no. 1917.815

As is often the case with antique art, some controversy surrounds the Wadsworth Atheneum's famous cloaked warrior. Problems of dating, hand, tradition, style, and authenticity are not uncommon, and since this particular piece has unique characteristics, it has proved especially problematic. Most likely, this statuette is from the archaic period, dating from the late sixth century B.C., and may have been executed in the Peloponnese. It portrays a Greek warrior, most likely a hoplite (a foot soldier), who wears a cloak and a Corinthian helmet. While there are many such representations of foot soldiers in antique art, the Wadsworth's warrior is characterized by two peculiar features: the transverse crest and a cloak which nearly completely covers the body. That these two traits appear in the same work seems even more idiosyncratic.

Much of the scholarly history of this piece is discussed in Joan R. Merten's article "A Greek Bronze Statuette in the Wadsworth Atheneum" published in *Bulletin of the Wadsworth Atheneum* in winter 1968. It is more appropriate here to describe the magnetic strength of its formal qualities. Although it stands less than eight inches high, the statuette possesses a monumental power and its most remarkable characteristic is its striking assertion of geometric shape. This results primarily from the subordination of details to the broader volumes and masses of the piece. Most stunning is the severe angle leading from the warrior's left leg and arm to his right leg and arm. This dramatic cut, combined with another sharp angle formed by a plane leading from the right shoulder through the elbow into the forearm and then the leg, creates a complex yet legible geometric volume. There is, however, a degree of detailed description in this statuette, with insistent rhythms established by drapery folds which reemphasize the dramatic and sweeping angles of the piece. Furthermore, the stylized helmet and braids function as a complex foil to the reduced planes of the hoplite's helmet, which imbue this common foot soldier with a certain ferocity and brutal anonymity.

The powerful geometry of the sculpture seems even more impressive today because so much of the best contemporary architecture and sculpture reflects a similar concern with geometry and shape. In this context, it is worth considering the relationship between the forms of this sixth century B.C. statuette and those of another sculpture in the Wadsworth Atheneum's collection—Tony Smith's completely non-representational, monumental eleven-foot-high and geometric *Amaryllis* of 1965.

17

WORKSHOP OF FRA ANGELICO

Head of an Angel

Ca. 1438–40
Tempera on panel
17.1 x 13.9 cm. (6 3/4 x 5 1/2 in.)
The Ella Gallup Sumner and
  Mary Catlin Sumner Collection
Acquisition no. 1928.321

Attributions concerning the art of Fra Angelico have been problematic. Although there is a significant body of work securely assigned to this Renaissance master, difficulties have arisen because of misconceptions about the true nature of Fra Angelico's art. Traditionally, Angelico has been thought of as an artist whose main charms lay in his *retardataire* characteristics rather than his revolutionary ones. His sweet colors, decorative surfaces, and gentle figures implied to many the continuation of a late Gothic tradition. While these qualities are a part of much of Angelico's work, what is sometimes overlooked is his mastery of perspective, his complete understanding of the spatial and volumetric potential of light and shade and the convincing anatomy of many of his figures. As a result, Angelico's art should be understood as fundamental to the revolutionary currents in the Renaissance, akin to the work of such innovative contemporaries as Masaccio. Even so, Masaccio's robustness or even crudeness is completely alien to the delicacy and tranquility of Angelico.

Head of an Angel, which is a fragment of a larger panel of *The Madonna and Child* in the Rijksmuseum, Amsterdam, was executed by a follower of Fra Angelico; it has a sweetness and quietude typical of Angelico's art. The work also reveals the poetry resulting from a mixture of Gothic and Renaissance styles. The gold-leaf background and the delicate, refined handling of color, pattern, and texture appear to be Gothic holdovers. The Renaissance aspects of the piece are revealed primarily in the careful modelling of the face, in which subtle modulations of light and shade suggest plasticity and the revolution of form into depth.

19

PIERO DI COSIMO

b. Florence, 1462
d. Florence, 1521 (?)

The Finding of Vulcan on Lemnos

Ca. 1485–90
Oil on canvas
152.7 x 168.6 cm. (60 1/8 x 66 3/8)
The Ella Gallup Sumner and
   Mary Catlin Sumner Collection
Acquisition no. 1932.1

Controversy surrounds the career of Piero di Cosimo in general, and the Wadsworth Atheneum's *The Finding of Vulcan* in particular. Described by the Renaissance chronicler Vasari as an eccentric character, Piero di Cosimo forged a unique style that ran counter to the dominant current of the Italian Renaissance. Whereas qualities of naturalism, order, and idealism characterize the preeminent artists of the period, Piero di Cosimo pursued poetry and fantasy in his art. While he did paint serious themes, he favored primitive subjects such as stories of the Stone Age, and he populated his pieces with strangely sensuous figures, weird animals, and imaginative hybrids.

His canvases frequently contain charming and often well-rendered landscapes, but problems, or perhaps poetry, arise when he places inhabitants in these settings. Linearly modelled figures in brocaded, diaphanous garments recalling those of Botticelli, Signorelli, and Lippi appear sharply silhouetted or almost detached from their ground. Difficulties in scale and awkwardness of pose further complicate his pictures, though these oddities are often beguiling.

The Finding of Vulcan is part of a series of works on the history of primitive man, probably intended to decorate the palace of Francesco del Pugliese, a wealthy Florentine wool merchant. The scene shown here supposedly illustrates the moment after Vulcan has been cast off Mt. Olympus by his mother, Juno, who was repelled by her disfigured son. Upon landing, the god is discovered by a group of amused women, who offer aid to the awkward boy. Another interpretation of the painting also exists. For years it was assumed to be a scene of *Hylas and the Nymphs*. Hylas, a beautiful lad, who had gone to fetch water for Heracles, is discovered by nymphs, who become aroused and shower him with affection. Though the story of Vulcan is now commonly accepted as the theme of the piece, there is an inescapable air of eroticism created by the curious, half-clothed women, whose welcome appears to contain more allure than bemusement.

21

GERMAN

St. Michael

Ca. 1500
Polychromed and gilded wood
79.4 cm. high (31 1/4 in.)
J. J. Goodwin Fund
Acquisition no. 1932.294

The sculptor of this piece is unknown, but it appears to come from the stylistic tradition of Nicholas Gerhaert, who worked in various locales in Germany between 1462 and 1473. There is debate as to whether this sculpture was done in northern or southern Germany, but it recalls the work of Erasmus Grasser, who carved in a Gerhaertesque manner, in and around Munich between 1474 and 1518.

Polychromed wood sculpture enjoyed particular popularity in Germany in the late fifteenth and early sixteenth centuries. Although usually commissioned by the Church, such sculpture was often paid for by the local town councils, whose main members were wealthy burghers. Wood sculptures might be single, nearly life-size or half-size figures, or smaller statuettes. Often a complete altarpiece, or retable, as it was called, was carved in wood and comprised a sculptured ensemble which included figures.

St. Michael may have been a single figure, but most likely it was part of a specific altarpiece, either an occupant of one of its niches or as an attendant statue. St. Michael is the Captain General of Angels, whose major duties include the weighing and division of souls at the Last Judgment and the protection of the Church Militant against the forces of Satan. With his cloak of armor and his right hand raised and left lowered, he personifies both warrior and judge.

The charms of this work spring from its ingenious composition. The two nearly symmetrical wings, along with the base and the horizontally bent forearm, operate as a solid trapezoidal frame for the dynamic rhythms within. The right side of the figure is open with right arm thrusting upward while the left is closed, enveloped in a whirlpool of descending drapery. These motions may allude to souls that ascend toward heaven or are sucked down into hell. This eddy of drapery, combined with a series of intersecting diagonals, creates a sway and instability that evoke the oscillation of a balancing scale. As is typical of so much sculpture of this kind, wood is painted in beguiling hues: here, golds and blues are the dominant colors. Other engaging details include the sweet, beatific gaze of St. Michael, the stylized braids of his hair, and his elegant hipshot pose.

23

LUCAS CRANACH THE ELDER

b. Kronach, Upper Franconia, 1472
d. Weimar, 1553

The Feast of Herod

1531
Oil on panel
81.5 x 120 cm. (32 1/8 x 47 1/4 in.)
The Ella Gallup Sumner and
    Mary Catlin Sumner Collection
Acquisition no. 1936.339

Court painter to princes and friend of theologian Martin Luther, Lucas Cranach was one of Saxony's most respected artists and citizens. Throughout his life, he served in numerous political capacities. Late in his career, he established one of the most prolific artistic workshops, which produced portraits, religious and mythological themes, and female nudes that delighted his public and provided him with great wealth.

There is an irresistible charm to Cranach's quirky style. As we see in *The Feast of Herod*, he often places his figures against a dark background, and these individuals, whose contours are indicated by nervously, even awkwardly drawn lines, seem almost detached from their surrounding space. This quivering linearity runs wild throughout the work, enlivening drapery folds, stitching and brocading of clothing, curls of hair, and the surfaces of fruit. A viewpoint from above serves to compress the space, while it also provides a crucial overhead view of some of the most important and most gruesome details of the work. The obsessive linearism and the artist's tight space lend an air of unreality to the painting.

The theme of the piece, *The Feast of Herod*, deals with Salome's request for the head of St. John the Baptist as a reward for dancing for her stepfather, King Herod. Salome shocks the dinner party by bringing her spoils to the table. The carefully depicted head of the decapitated St. John, whose terrified eyes seem to stare at Salome, is one of Cranach's most accomplished passages of painting, and he cleverly contrasts it with a tray piled high with many fruits, the actual dessert of this repast.

Cranach's theme was one of a class of subjects, popular at the time, that demonstrated the dominance of woman; these included Samson and Delilah, Phyllis and Aristotle, and Judith and Holofernes. As is common in Cranach's work, his figures from the past often take on the features of his contemporaries: in this instance, King Herod is played by the recently deceased Frederick the Wise. Since Frederick had been Cranach's patron and friend, it is difficult in this case to interpret the artist's intention.

BRUSSELS

Hunting Scene

Ca. 1580
Tapestry: wool and silk
274.3 x 318.8 cm. (108 x 125 ½ in.)
Gift of Elisha E. Hilliard
Acquisition no. 1945.430

The hunting scene has a venerable tradition in the history of European tapestry. Hangings from the Middle Ages depict both mythical and prosaic hunts, and the theme was carried on through the Baroque era. One of the major Renaissance hunt cycles is Bernard van Orley's so-called *Great Hunts of Maximilian* (now scattered among several collections) of about 1535. Van Orley had travelled to Italy from his native Flanders; there he met Raphael, and his work shows a definite Italianate influence. In 1515 he was appointed to the Brussels guild and became court painter to Marguerite of Austria. His *Maximilian* tapestries show a variety of hunts, each one suited to a month of the year. They were woven in Brussels, and their vibrant realism set new standards for the genre. The flattened space and *mille-fleurs* decoration of earlier examples were replaced by principles of Renaissance perspective and naturalistic landscape.

The Brussels tapestry illustrated here is descended from Van Orley's model. However, where Van Orley was influenced by Italian art, the artist of this piece relies on a more Northern tradition. The arrangement of space and the abundant details reflect the work of artists like Cranach and Pieter Brueghel the Elder. The border is embellished with miniature scenes, *amorini*, flowers, and a number of allegorical figures typical of late sixteenth-century Flemish decorative art. For example, in the lower left corner are Mars and Venus, in the lower right Jupiter and Juno, and at the top center sits Charity. These details serve as an accompaniment to the central image, adding moral metaphors to the everyday scene of the hunt.

This composition is not unique. A Brussels hunt tapestry, formerly in the collection of Mrs. Gloria Morgan Vanderbilt, is identical in many respects, although it is clearly by another hand. The formal garden in the background of the Wadsworth Atheneum example is echoed in one of the seven *Fêtes of Henry III* tapestries, now in the Uffizi Gallery in Florence. Therefore, while these Brussels works could hardly be called mass-produced (it took well over a year to execute just one tapestry), it is clear that the sixteenth-century weaving shops shared a common set of patterns adaptable to assorted purposes.

A.L.G.

27

ATTRIBUTED TO CHRISTOPHE JAMNITZER

b. Nuremberg, 1563
d. Nuremberg, 1618

Cabinet

Ca. 1600
Oak, ebony, silver, and rock crystal
73.7 x 63.5 x 33 cm. (29 x 25 x
   13 in.)
Gift of J. Pierpont Morgan
Acquisition no. 1917.247

Christophe Jamnitzer was heir to the skills of one of the finest goldsmithing families in Germany. Wenzel Jamnitzer, Christophe's grandfather, founded the family trade that was carried on by his brother, son, nephew, and grandson. The Jamnitzers worked in a rich Mannerist style with a vocabulary derived from the Italian Renaissance.

This chest is typical of the Jamnitzer canon. Its overall decoration is closely related to Wenzel's famous silver casket now in the Munich Residenzmuseum. However, the twisting posture of the figures and the proportions of the architectural details point to Christophe as the author of this piece. More generally, the intricately worked silver and elongated scheme of the design, in which grace rather than monumentality rules, is typical of the late Mannerist art of Germany at the close of the sixteenth century.

The theme of this decoration appears to be imperial authority. The upper central figure seated on a throne, framed by a *trompe l'oeil* niche, has been identified as the Hapsburg emperor. Below are seated Hope and Justice on either side of Jupiter. On each of the inner faces of the wings, the emperor reappears, surmounted on the left by Temperance, on the right by Faith. Further allegorical and mythological details amplify this vision of almost divine leadership. Yet the quality of the execution prevents this piece from being merely didactic. The figures strike attitudes, but they seem imbued with a spirit of fantasy rather than of law. Works such as this represent the last flowering of Renaissance art in Germany. The Thirty Years' War, beginning in 1618, devastated the country, and it was not until the middle of the eighteenth century that this level of craftsmanship was once again achieved.

A.L.G.

29

LONDON

Mostyn Steeple Cup

1613
Gilded silver
62.9 cm. high (24 3/4 in.)
Elizabeth B. Miles Collection
Acquisition no. 1979.144

It was to Germany that English silversmiths looked during the reigns of Elizabeth I and James I, and the craftsmen of Augsburg and Nuremburg dominated the Northern market of finely worked silver and gold. English decorative arts, by comparison, lagged somewhat behind. However, the steeple cup, so named for its long, steeple-shaped lid, was an English innovation. It evolved from the German standing cups (cups capped by standing figures); but where the German cups tended toward low and broad proportions, the English version became highly attenuated, taking the Mannerist aesthetic to its logical extreme.

The cup in the Wadsworth Atheneum is an exceptional example of early seventeenth-century silver. The maker's mark is "T.C.," and it was made in London in 1613. The superabundance of ornament gives the piece an animated appearance with each varied facet capturing and reflecting light. It was meant to contain wine, and was made for the Mostyn family of Flintshire, North Wales—a family already in possession of the noted Mostyn Hall plate of 1586–87. That earlier Elizabethan silver service set a high standard for this steeple cup to match. While the later piece must have been executed by another hand (and is a generation later in its overall design and style), it shows the same vocabulary of repoussé embellishment, including the seried ovals, arms, and animals. The main theme of the steeple cup decoration is nautical; dolphin-like creatures, both incised and raised, encircle the cup repeatedly, and form a lively counterpoint to the imposing architectural framework of the piece.

A.L.G.

31

SEBASTIANO DEL PIOMBO

b. Venice, ca. 1485
d. Rome, 1547

Man in Armor

Ca. 1511–15
Oil on canvas
87.6 x 66.7 cm. (34 1/2 x 26 1/4 in.)
The Ella Gallup Sumner and
   Mary Catlin Sumner Collection
Acquisition no. 1960.119

Tremendous power and force characterize Sebastiano del Piombo's *Man in Armor*. Although identification of the figure as the heroic Florentine captain Francesco Ferucci is uncertain, the figure possesses a determination, tinged with ferocity, that elevates it to epic realms. Sebastiano achieves this level of intensity through a portrayal that combines the best of the Venetian and Roman High Renaissance heritages. Born in Venice, Sebastiano was first exposed to the work of Giovanni Bellini, Giorgione, and Titian, and later, after settling in Rome in 1511, came under the influence of Raphael and Michelangelo.

This variety of inspirations produces a heady mix in the *Man in Armor*. From the Venetians, Sebastiano developed his atmospheric colors, evidenced in the dusky olives and rusts of the background and the ruddy glow of the warrior's flesh. Venetian concern for texture is brilliantly displayed in the flash of light that illuminates the soldier's armor. Moreover, the pose of the torso-length figure, with his arm resting on a support or a balustrade and his crooked elbow appearing perilously close to the picture plane, echoes another Venetian formula.

His assimilation of Roman style is revealed in the intelligent massing of volumes, recalling Raphael's work, and the monumental energy of the figure, reminiscent of Michelangelo. Sebastiano both structures and stimulates the painting with masterful compositional rhymes and counterpoints. The head is cocked in a direction opposite to the thrust of his forearm, but the diagonal tilt of the head is echoed in the weapon he holds. The dazzling, armor-covered elbow, the element closest to the picture plane, is the launching point for two key movements, one across the arm and hand, the other up into his face and head, with its wild hair and scruffy beard. Sebastiano thus links the fierce convictions of the warrior with the physical instruments that execute these convictions.

33

JACOPO BASSANO

b. Bassano del Grappa, ca. 1516
d. Bassano del Grappa, 1592

**The Mystic Marriage of
St. Catherine**

Ca. 1550
Oil on canvas
89.5 x 112.1 cm. (35 1/4 x 44 1/8 in.)
The Ella Gallup Sumner and
  Mary Catlin Sumner Collection
Acquisition no. 1959.254

The strangeness infusing Jacopo Bassano's *The Mystic Marriage of St. Catherine* is symptomatic of a great deal of Italian art of the *Cinquecento*. The extreme attenuation of the figures, the odd mixture of pale and intense colors, the crowded space of the foreground plane leaping without much middle ground into depth, and the confusing criss-cross of compositional movements all identify this distinctive sixteenth-century style. Customarily called Mannerism, this tendency has been variously explained. One of its definitions refers to an involvement with the manner of Michelangelo; that is, admirers of Michelangelo attempted to outdo his qualities of muscularity, emotion, drama, and tension. As Mannerist art departed further and further from realism, it developed an idealism and individuality that could suggest elegance and stylishness on the one hand, and spirituality and otherworldliness on the other. Its grace struck a sympathetic chord with an increasingly courtly society, while its bizarreness aptly reflected a society suffering a spiritual crisis. Furthermore, the idiosyncrasies of Mannerist art satisfied a demand for art of technical virtuosity.

The Mystic Marriage of St. Catherine demonstrates this Mannerist sensibility. Figures are elongated yet muscular, colors range from pale crimsons to rich oranges, brushstroke is liberated and active, drapery folds are dynamic, and space and composition are confusing, almost turbulent. Some of the spatial distortions may be attributed to the fact that this piece is cut down from a larger canvas. But the overall aura of the work implies eccentricity, and though it owes something to the painters of the Venetian High Renaissance, the influence of the archetypal Mannerist Parmagianino is unquestionable, especially in Bassano's depiction of a column-necked leading lady. Moreover, Bassano's distinctive style proved to be a stimulus to the Spanish painter El Greco.

The subject is St. Catherine of Alexandria, a brilliant and beautiful woman who insisted on remaining single until the truly perfect prince arrived. Informed by an old hermit that Christ would court her if she converted to Christianity, Catherine became a believer after Christ appeared to her in a dream and placed a ring on her finger. The patron saint of girls, Catherine is also the subject of another painting in the Wadsworth Atheneum by Bernardo Strozzi, who portrays her with the attributes of her martyrdom.

35

MICHELANGELO MERISI
DA CARAVAGGIO

b. Caravaggio, Italy 1573
d. Porto Ercole, Italy 1610

Ecstasy of St. Francis

Ca. 1594
Oil on canvas
92.4 x 127.6 cm. (36 3/8 x 50 1/4 in.)
The Ella Gallup Sumner and
    Mary Catlin Sumner Collection
Acquisition no. 1943.222

Michelangelo da Caravaggio was one of Italy's greatest artists, and *Ecstasy of St. Francis* is one of the museum's most prized possessions. It dates from Caravaggio's earliest period in Rome and may well be his first piece to include a landscape. The story probably portrays the moment after St. Francis received the stigmata; he swoons in ecstasy, supported by an angel. Departing from traditional representations of this scene, in which a vision of Christ appears in the sky and rays emanate from his body to that of St. Francis, Caravaggio gives us several thin slivers of light as an indication of Christ's presence. Thus, light, in and of itself, carries divine power.

Because Caravaggio preferred to suggest divinity through naturalistic means, he has been called a realist artist. Realism for him, however, did not mean a slavish imitation of nature. Rather, it meant avoiding idealism, and Caravaggio's innovation was in bringing spiritual subject matter down to the level of the spectator. Tangibility of imagery increased accessibility; in this fashion, Caravaggio's art functions as a pictorial equivalent to the ideas in St. Ignatius Loyola's *Spiritual Exercises*. Loyola's writings, popular in Rome at this time, stress the simplification of devotion through an individual's direct contact with God via faith.

The physicality of images in *The Ecstasy of St. Francis* is apparent. Well modelled figures, placed close to the picture plane, almost impinge on the viewer's space, and the background is dusky and amorphous. (Note, in particular, the knee of the angel and the hand of St. Francis, which nearly puncture the plane of the canvas.) The power of facial expression, another aspect of Caravaggio's realism, is evident in the beatific gaze of St. Francis and the sweet physiognomy of the angel.

Dark olives and browns permeate the piece, but animation is added through bold chiaroscuro. This dramatic contrast of light and dark is known as tenebrism, a term used specifically to describe Caravaggio's approach. His tenebrism influenced a generation of European artists (Rembrandt is the most famous of these), and interactions between light and dark, exploited for a variety of purposes, became a trademark of the Baroque style.

ORAZIO GENTILESCHI

b. Pisa, 1565
d. London, 1647

**Judith and the Maidservant
with the Head of Holofernes**

Ca. 1610–12
Oil on canvas
133.2 x 156.8 cm. (52 $7/16$ x
61 $3/4$ in.)
The Ella Gallup Sumner and
Mary Catlin Sumner Collection
Acquisition no. 1949.52

Like many of Italy's better Baroque painters, Orazio Gentileschi was strongly influenced by the work of Caravaggio. Of the many *Caravaggisti*, Gentileschi was one of the most accomplished, and occasionally his works achieve a poetic power akin to that of his master. *Judith and the Maidservant with the Head of Holofernes* is one such work.

This piece, painted between 1610 and 1612, is brilliantly composed. Placed against a nearly coal-black ground is a riveting pyramidal configuration of forms. At its apex are the two sharply lit faces, which look in opposite directions, gazing intently, mindful of threat and discovery. A line flows from each of their heads, through their shoulders and arms, and meets at the basket that cradles the severed head of Holofernes. There is a disturbing poignancy in the position of the head between Judith and the executioner and her accomplice, an intimate arrangement reminiscent of a mother holding her baby. Yet, emanating from the ellipse of heads and hands is the sword that carried out the horrible deed, masterfully projected toward the viewer's space, reminding him of the gruesomeness of this event. The bottom portions of the women's gowns constitute the base of the pyramid, providing a solid foundation for the more dynamic elements above. This mixture of elegance and doom is amplified in the colors of the canvas from its deep blacks to its vibrant reds, golds, and blues.

Caravaggesque in its dramatic lighting, expressive faces, active forms, and concern with texture, *Judith and the Maidservant with the Head of Holofernes* also has an elegance characteristic of Gentileschi's work, and the blend of these ingredients produces an arresting brew. The subject of Judith decapitating Holofernes in order to save her town was one of several popular themes illustrating the power of women. It is worth noting, in this context, that Orazio's daughter Artemesia, who also was a painter, was attracted to such themes, and these have frequently been interpreted by critics as significant feminist statements.

BERNARDO STROZZI

b. Genoa, 1581
d. Venice, 1644

St. Catherine of Alexandria

Ca. 1631–44
Oil on canvas
154.3 x 66.3 cm. (60 3/4 x 26 1/8 in.)
The Ella Gallup Sumner and Mary
    Catlin Sumner Collection
Acquisition no. 1931.99

The birth of Protestantism rocked the Roman Catholic Church. In response, the papacy launched the Counter-Reformation to recapture those who had left the fold and to reinforce the faith of potentially wavering adherents. One by-product of the Counter-Reformation was a shift in emphasis in religious iconography to subjects intended to appeal to the faith and emotions of its audiences: thus, martyrdom and the miracles of Christ and the saints came to dominate Italian art of the late sixteenth and the seventeenth centuries—the period of the Baroque.

St. Catherine was a wealthy and educated noblewoman living in Alexandria in the third century A.D. She outspokenly defended the Christians who were to be put to death by Maxentius II. For her efforts, she was condemned to die by starvation. But St. Catherine's will, both spiritual and corporeal, was not easily destroyed. Angels delivered food to her cell, preventing her death, so her tormentors decided to torture her on a spiked wheel. But Catherine again prevailed: a fireball from heaven exploded the wheel and spikes and also consumed her executioners. Finally, Catherine's assassins succeeded in beheading her. Her faith and extraordinary multiple salvations resulted in her canonization.

Bernardo Strozzi represents a seated St. Catherine and in the customary fashion of depicting martyrs, has her holding the instruments of her torture, in this case, several spikes and a broken wheel. Her sweet face suggests her charity, and her voluminous form, accented by jagged, wrinkled drapery folds, implies her indomitable spirit. Her foot on the Bible indicates the strength provided through faith.

Although it is uncertain when Strozzi painted this piece, its luminosity and jewellike array of lavender, aquamarine, turquoise, and ivory colors place it in his Venetian period, between 1631 and 1644. Born in Genoa, Strozzi entered the Capuchin order in the Monastery of Santa Barbara around 1597. To provide for his family, however, he left the order, for there was more wealth to be had in painting the religious life than in leading it. Upon the death of his mother in 1630, Strozzi was expected to rejoin the order, but art and the secular way of life had established their appeal. Although the details of this period of his life are unclear, it seems that Strozzi fled Genoa, after having been jailed for disobedience. Genoa's loss was Venice's gain, for Strozzi's art now reflected a vitality and dazzle inspired by the great Venetian colorists Tintoretto, Titian, and Veronese.

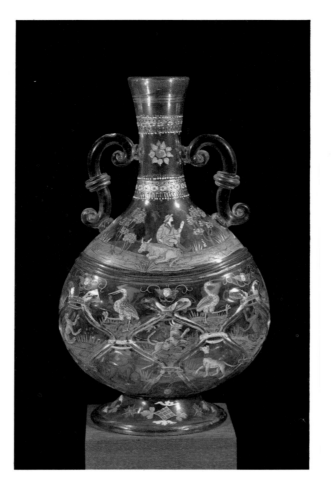

VENICE(?)

Pilgrim Flask

Ca. 1500–25
Blown, enamelled, and gilded glass
37.8 cm. high (14 7/8 in.)
Gift of J. Pierpont Morgan
Acquisition no. 1917.336

This flask was probably made in Venice, the great center of European glass-making. Here we see all aspects of the glass-worker's art; the finely blown shape, the gracefully modelled scroll handles, the applied bands, and the brilliant array of gilded and enamelled motifs all demonstrate the range of Renaissance imagination and design. The overall shape of this flask, flattened rather than cylindrical, is derived from the ceramic water and ointment bottles that wandering pilgrims hung about their necks. However, this delicate masterpiece was never meant to be taken on a journey to a shrine in Spain or Jerusalem; the pilgrim design was used rather as a starting point for the glass blower's fantasy. At the same time the theme of pilgrimage is alluded to wittily by the landscape on the neck of the flask, in which a traveller appears to be in the midst of a comic adventure.

A.L.G.

VENICE(?)

Two Goblets

Seventeenth century(?)
Blown and colored glass
Left: 22.2 cm. high (8 ¾ in.)
Right: 24.1 cm. high (9 ½ in.)
Gift of J. Pierpont Morgan
Acquisition nos. 1917.341, 345

Venice became the center of the European glass-making industry in the thirteenth century; major factories were established in Murano (a Venetian island) in 1291, and even today most of the world's finest works in glass are produced there. One of the results of this long-established tradition is that over the centuries glass-workers felt called upon to experiment to discover new and unusual forms. These two goblets present a particularly charming example of fanciful decoration. The stems of the glasses have virtually put forth flowers, and blossoms and leaves spring out with the elastic energy of natural growth. This kind of work is typical of Venetian glassware in the seventeenth century, when, as now, they were considered the finest of collector's items.

A.L.G.

43

FRANCISCO DE ZURBARÁN

b. Fuente de Cantos, 1598
d. Madrid, 1664

St. Serapio

1628
Oil on canvas
120.8 x 104.3 cm. (47 9/16 x 41 in.)
Anonymous gift
Acquisition no. 1939.479

Peter Serapio was an English monk who suffered a gruesome martyrdom at the hands of the Moors in 1240. As a member of the order of the Calced Mercedarians, St. Serapio became the subject of one of a series of works by Francisco de Zurbarán for the Monastery of Our Lady of Ransom (a Mercedarian order) located in Seville. Zurbarán is best known for his striking religious images, and the *St. Serapio* at the Atheneum might well have been a trial piece executed to display his prowess to his commissioners. This powerful work, done early in Zurbarán's career, before much of his art grew painterly and sentimental, achieves its strength from its sobriety and starkness. The figure of St. Serapio hangs against a dark, nearly amorphous background. His harshly lighted habit contains a brilliant, nearly abstract arrangement of starchy folds, suggesting Zurbarán's interest in sculpture. The head rests weightily on his shoulders, eyelids are heavily closed, the mouth is puffed and slightly pursed, and his hands are still and lifeless following his ordeal. All elements contribute to the sense of suffering of this Christian martyr. There is no respite from the severe image; the body occupies nearly the entire composition and there is little other pictorial incident to provide relief or distraction. Predominantly beige and brown in hue, the painting of St. Serapio contains two identifying marks—a contrasting red clasp with the symbol of his order, and a *trompe l'oeil* rendition of a scrap of paper which bears his name and appears to be affixed to the canvas. Like most of Zurbarán's best work, *St. Serapio* achieves its depth of spirituality through the intensity of its realism.

45

JUSEPE DE RIBERA

b. Jative, 1588
d. Naples, 1656

The Sense of Taste

Ca. 1635
Oil on canvas
113.7 x 87.6 cm. (44 3/4 x 34 1/2 in.)
The Ella Gallup Sumner and
  Mary Catlin Sumner Collection
Acquisition no. 1963.194

The influence of the famous early Italian Baroque painter Michelangelo da Caravaggio was so profound that a whole generation of his followers became known as the *Caravaggisti*. One such disciple was Jusepe de Ribera (known as Il Spagnoletto, the little Spaniard), whose date of arrival in Italy is uncertain but who settled in Naples around 1616. His earliest works demonstrate his borrowing from and intensification of Caravaggio's style. In the hands of Ribera, Caravaggio's sharp chiaroscuro, dramatic foreshortening, and expressive features are vehemently amplified. Oppositions of light and dark are tense and explosive, foreshortening is unstable, often vertiginous, and features are frequently violently contorted. However, as Ribera's art matured, many of these aggressive tendencies were stilled and his art takes on a humility and temperateness.

Religious scenes constitute the bulk of Ribera's output, but *The Sense of Taste*, part of a series on the five senses painted in Rome, was not an uncommon theme for contemporary artists. Until recently, the attribution of the Wadsworth Atheneum's *The Sense of Taste* was unclear, but new evidence places it within the oeuvre of Ribera. What is unique about his treatment of the subject is its representation in vernacular, almost vulgar terms. Customarily, the five senses were portrayed through erudite symbolism or veiled allegories: here Ribera, in the tradition of Caravaggio's realism, brings the subject down to the most common level. Taste is illustrated by a crude, corpulent man, mouth opened and skewed, seemingly overwhelmed by what he should consume next. On a table, close to the picture plane, sits his repast; with one hand, he holds a wine glass, and with the other, he clutches a flask of wine. Light-dark contrasts, along with the spontaneous expression of the figure, who tipsily holds the goblet and the tipped wine bottle, are all in keeping with a lively Baroque portrayal. The works of the rest of the series are similar to *The Sense of Taste*: each consists of a single figure, placed behind a table on which rests an object suggestive of its theme. Most amusing is *The Sense of Smell* (present location unknown), in which another somewhat dishevelled man holds up onions and garlic for display.

SALVATOR ROSA

b. Naples, 1615
d. Rome, 1673

La Ricciardi, Mistress of the Artist, as a Sybil

Ca. 1640
Oil on canvas
115.9 x 94 cm. (45 5/8 x 37 in.)
The Ella Gallup Sumner and
   Mary Catlin Sumner Collection
Acquisition no. 1956.159

Though he painted during the Baroque era in Italy, Salvator Rosa was something of a Renaissance man. In addition to being a painter, he was an accomplished poet, actor, musician, and engraver. Flamboyant and colorful, Rosa stirred controversy wherever he went. Born in Naples into an artistic family, he spent time in Rome in the 1630s, where he staged a satire attacking Bernini. Rosa's barbs were received with hostility, and he moved to the more congenial atmosphere of Florence. There he established the *Accademia dei Percossi*, an erudite group of Tuscan intellectuals.

La Ricciardi, Mistress of the Artist was probably executed in Florence in the 1640s. A pendant to his own self-portrait, now in the National Gallery in London, this piece portrays his mistress, Lucrezia Paolina del fu Silvestro, in the guise of a muse or sybil. Always provocative, Rosa flaunts his mistress before the eyes of the public. Rosa's works are genuinely unique for the period; their golden, glowing tones, spiralling movements, and intense, rebellious, slightly sinister figures foretoken the Romantic age. Represented as a muse, Lucrezia, with her dishevelled hair and scarf, and her twisting posture, seems more Bohemian than classical. The unorthodoxy of Rosa's art is precisely what appealed to later generations, particularly those artists interested in the awesome and the sublime.

49

PETER PAUL RUBENS

b. Siegen, Germany, 1577
d. Antwerp, 1640

The Return of the Holy Family from Egypt

Ca. 1613
Oil on canvas
231.5 x 153 cm. (91 1/8 x 60 1/4 in.)
The Ella Gallup Sumner and
   Mary Catlin Sumner Collection
Acquisition no. 1938.254

Under Spanish domination, Flanders in the sixteenth century became a stronghold of Catholicism against the rising tide of Protestantism in the north and west of Europe. As was the case throughout Catholic Europe, the Church, in its attempt to reconvert heteroclites and to reaffirm the faith of its adherents, used art as a means of carrying its messages. The Counter-Reformation spirit was embodied in Baroque art, which stressed faith as a central doctrine and exalted the power of the Catholic Church.

Born a Lutheran and later a devout convert to Catholicism, Peter Paul Rubens was Flanders's leading Baroque painter and one of its most erudite scholars and accomplished diplomats. If the Baroque style implies theatricality, energy, and ecstasy, then Rubens was perhaps the most Baroque artist of all. Intense, dramatic, and vibrant, Rubens's art contains archetypal Baroque characteristics: grand scale, diagonal movements into space, curvilinear activity on the canvas surface, brilliant colorism, liberated brushstroke, explosive chiaroscuro, and robust, dynamic figures.

Like many northern painters, Rubens developed his style under the tutelage of Italian art. He learned tenebrism from Caravaggio, vivid colorism from the Venetians, and expressive figuration from Michelangelo. His large painting *The Return of the Holy Family from Egypt* demonstrates some of these characteristics. Voluminous figures are placed on a diagonal into space, and drapery swirls, rich hues, sumptuous textures, and areas of active brushstroke enliven the piece. Some of the religious weightiness of the painting, however, seems lightened by the garb of the Virgin, which, in its fashionableness, suggests a lady out for an afternoon stroll rather than a participant in a holy event.

51

JUAN DE VALDES LEAL

b. Seville, 1622
d. Seville, 1690

Vanitas

1660
Oil on canvas
130.7 x 99.4 cm. (51 7/16 x 39 1/8 in.)
The Ella Gallup Sumner and
  Mary Catlin Sumner Collection
Acquisition no. 1939.270

The *Vanitas* painting was a common religious motif which was particularly popular among Northern European artists during the Baroque period. The message of *Vanitas* art is that the value and beauty of material goods are merely fleeting; eventually they disappear and their possessors or admirers die. Only the spirit and soul live on. Thus, one should care for and cultivate the spiritual rather than the material.

What is intriguing about *Vanitas* pieces is that they allow both artist and collector to "have it both ways," so to speak, reveling in images of opulent materiality, while seeming to condemn such images. These works are normally rife with things of great beauty, albeit often slightly in decay. Thus the artist could depict splendid objects and display his technical virtuosity while still adhering to religious and moral principles.

Juan de Valdes Leal was one of Spain's leading Baroque painters. Religious paintings were his prime subjects, and he was particularly preoccupied with themes of death and martyrdom. Mortality is again his concern in this *Vanitas*. It is an overwhelming work, chock-full of objects, rich in color, and laden with symbolism. Among the more typical items in this canvas are a candle and watch implying the transience of time, and flowers, which suggest that beauty fades. Crowns and a scepter signify power, and coins and jewelry symbolize luxury and ultimate materiality. Of course, all are earthly objects whose value dissolves with death—a message made emphatic by the presence of a skull. Books were common in such depictions, generally with titles that contained discussions of vanity, but here the artist has varied from tradition. Instead, the subject of one of these volumes is the practice of art, next to which are placed the artist's tools. Though it is possible to see these as but another example of ephemeral worldly products, perhaps Valdes Leal is suggesting the immortal potential of art. At the left, a *putto* blows a bubble, demonstrating the fragility of the apparently tangible, and an angel reveals a Last Judgment painting, the definitive treatise on the importance of the spiritual.

53

FRANS HALS

b. Antwerp, 1581/1595 (?)
d. Haarlem, 1666

Joseph Coymans

1644
Oil on canvas
84 x 70 cm. (33 x 27 ½ in.)
The Ella Gallup Sumner and
  Mary Catlin Sumner Collection
Acquisition no. 1958.176

The rise in economic power of the middle class in Holland and the development of Protestantism, which generally shunned religious imagery, caused major transformations in seventeenth-century Dutch art. Since the church was no longer the primary art sponsor, and wealthier members of the middle class now could be patrons themselves, a shift in the subjects of art occurred. Obviously, religious painting became less important. Instead, individuals began to commission works to adorn their homes and offices, and artists responded by specializing in entertaining and attractive themes of genre, still life, landscapes, and portraiture. Portraits of the nouveau riche became popular. These portraits could be of single individuals, husband and wife, or when the cost of hiring a top artist grew too high, of groups. The group portrait, which was generally determined by the profession of the sitters, also held an appeal for a society in which status was defined more by occupation than by nobility of birth.

The portrait of *Joseph Coymans* is dated 1644, and it demonstrates Hals's unique style, in which a bravura brush fired his figures with animation and vitality. The coat of arms on the wall containing three cows refers to the name Coymans, which translates to "cowmans" although the family fortune derived from textiles and banking.

MICHAEL SWEERTS

b. Brussels, Belgium, 1624
d. Goa (Portuguese India), 1664

Boy with a Hat

Ca. 1655–60
Oil on canvas
37 x 29.5 cm. (14 1/2 x 11 5/8 in.)
The Ella Gallup Sumner and
　Mary Catlin Sumner Collection
Acquisition no. 1940.198

Michael Sweerts worked in Rome, Amsterdam, and his native city of Brussels. and died while he was en route to India with a party of missionaries. He was associated with the *Bamboccianti*, a group of Northern artists who specialized in humble genre scenes. His portraits of young boys, by virtue of their mundane costumes, suggest that these paintings were not commissioned, but were portrayals of a class or type in society. His *Boy with a Hat* is acknowledged as one of his most accomplished works. The canvas is characterized by gentle modulations of light and shade and a crystalline clarity. The boy's face, winsome and delicate, is blushed with a faint pink glow, and his golden hair and whitish collar are described by wispy, refined brushstrokes. Most striking are the youth's eyes, with their dewy sparkle and wistful focus on a distant object. There is a quality of stillness to this portrait that reminds most observers of Vermeer's masterful figural pieces, though there seems to be no documented connection between the two artists.

JACOB VAN RUISDAEL

b. Amsterdam, 1628/29
d. Haarlem, 1682

Bleaching Grounds
Near Haarlem

Ca. 1660 (?)
Oil on canvas
34 x 41.6 cm. (13 3/8 x 16 3/8 in.)
The Ella Gallup Sumner and
   Mary Catlin Sumner Collection
Acquisition no. 1950.498

With the rise of Protestantism, which avoided religious imagery, and the development of a wealthier middle class in seventeenth-century Holland, patronage of the arts shifted from the Church to merchants and professionals, and themes in art grew more secular. Among the most popular new subjects was landscape, and a battery of specialized artists emerged to satisfy the needs of the marketplace.

Since landscapes had previously occupied a lowly position in the hierarchy of acceptable subject matter, many of these masters sought ways of enhancing the role of this motif. Landscape could be elevated in several ways: it could serve as a backdrop for events from religion or mythology; it could be inhabited by ruins, consciously structured so as to suggest the classical or pastoral ideal; or its distinctive elements, such as weather and light, could be dramatically emphasized. In the case of Jacob van Ruisdael, one of Holland's popular landscape artists, the scene was most frequently presented with great honesty and forthrightness. But even Ruisdael did not avoid altering the arrangement of nature to intensify the compositional powers of his pictures.

For instance, in *Bleaching Grounds Near Haarlem*, a firm pictorial armature is provided both by a low horizon, slicing the work in two, and by the emphatic lines of the land, formed by irrigation ditches and roads. Functioning like the diagonals in a perspective system, these lines converge at the firmament toward the left side of the work and are there met by a wedge of clouds, the brightness of which mirrors the diagonals of the earth.

The view is spacious and panoramic, and this openness is characteristic of Ruisdael's late work. Light and atmosphere are well rendered, and alternations between bright and dark lend both drama and organization to the canvas. The clouds and sky are particularly expressive, undoubtedly reflecting their visual importance in low-lying Holland. Though the importance of the subject seems marginal in comparison with the sweep of nature, it is worth noting that Ruisdael chooses to represent the production of goods, in this case, the bleaching of linens, an activity of the sort that provided the wealth of the new class of art collectors.

57

NICOLAES BERCHEM

b. Haarlem, 1620
d. Amsterdam, 1683

A Moor Presenting a Parrot to a Lady

Ca. 1665
Oil on canvas
93.7 x 88.9 cm. (36 7/8 x 35 in.)
The Ella Gallup Sumner and
   Mary Catlin Sumner Collection
Acquisition no. 1961.29

Son of the famous Dutch still-life painter Pieter Claesz., Nicolaes Berchem was a prolific and popular painter of a wide variety of subjects. His oeuvre includes battles, harbor scenes, mythology, and history, but his most admired themes were Italian pastoral landscapes. Berchem understood the new class of art buyers emerging in seventeenth-century Holland, who did not want to be instructed in, or perhaps bothered by, scenes of religion and morality. They preferred portraits of themselves, diverting landscapes, genre and still lifes, and frequently themes of exoticism, sensuality, and fantasy.

Berchem's *A Moor Presenting a Parrot to a Lady* is a technically dazzling work on a gay and sensuous theme. Here, Berchem cleverly concocts a winning recipe to engage the public's fascination. The scene is set in what appears to be Naples, appealing to a love of Italy and interest in the activity of the harbors. The gift-bearing Moor adds a touch of exoticism, and the luxuriously bedecked lady, whose stance is echoed by the statue of Venus nearby, contributes the proper dash of romance. This coy mixture is also a pretext for Berchem's display of his artistic virtuosity. Contrasting textures abound: note the smooth satin of the young lady's gown, the feathers of the parrot, the fur of the dogs, the cool marble of statuary and architecture, the hard metal of the sword and lance, to mention but a few. Against the background of slate, pale blue, and grey is a profusion of brilliant aquamarines, vermillions, and golds. Amidst the pictorial riot, there is even a beautifully rendered still life. In many Dutch paintings of the period, objects had symbolic values. Here, the parrot, appropriately, signifies luxury.

59

SIMON VOUET

b. Paris, 1590
d. Paris, 1649

St. Margaret

Ca. 1620
Oil on canvas
99.1 x 74.3 cm. (39 x 29 1/4 in.)
The Ella Gallup Sumner and
   Mary Catlin Sumner Collection
Acquisition no. 1961.471

Simon Vouet was born in France and spent the formative years of his career in Italy. Around 1627, he returned to his native land, where he soon became one of the country's leading artists. Like the art of his rival Nicolas Poussin, Vouet's work is an amalgam of a variety of Italian Baroque and French classical styles. While with Poussin the scales tipped more toward the classical, Vouet leaned toward the Baroque, influenced by numerous artists from Caravaggio and the Caracci to lesser-knowns such as Lanfranco and Guercino.

In the spirit of the Baroque, Vouet selected a theme of the miraculous in his *St. Margaret*. Obviously, the power of faith is the message of the painting because Margaret holds a cross as her sole weapon against the grisly serpent. St. Margaret is one of Vouet's typical plump, yet sensual female figures. The somewhat sleepy allure of her face is contrasted with the riot of Baroque spirals that enswirl her body. The open-jawed snout of the monster at the lower left seems to break through the picture plane, and his head begins the compositional eddies that envelop the piece. The violent whirlpools of iridescent red, blue, and tan drapery are charged with a ferocity akin to that of the dragon, and agitated light and dark interactions further promote the drama. Vouet cleverly opposes this dizzying coil of activity with both St. Margaret's calm, dreamy expression and the delicate way she holds the triumphant cross.

CLAUDE LORRAIN

b. Chamagne, 1600
d. Rome, 1682

Saint George and the Dragon

Ca. 1643
Oil on canvas
148.6 x 111.7 cm. (58 1/2 x 44 in.)
The Ella Gallup Sumner and Mary
    Catlin Sumner Collection
Acquisition no. 1937.2

Claude Lorrain's *Saint George and the Dragon* serves a special purpose in the collection of the Wadsworth Atheneum. Not only is it a fine example of Claude's distinctive landscape style, it is also representative of the kind of work that greatly influenced later generations of landscape artists, especially those of the Hudson River School, whose paintings are also among the great riches of the Museum.

What attracted the Hudson River School, particularly Thomas Cole, to Claude, was his elevation of landscape to a significant mode in art. Since the Hudson River artists were intent on making native landscape their primary artistic subject, they looked to Claude for inspiration, for he had developed "conventions" that imbued landscape with the qualities of respectable art.

These conventions are readily recognizable in *Saint George and the Dragon*. The most significant of these is the *repoussoir* technique, in which tall trees and rocks are placed at either edge of the picture, "framing" the work and establishing the picture plane from which the other elements develop in space. This sense of framing is enhanced by a dark foreground that causes the central scoop of the canvas to appear highlighted. As is customary, the middle ground contains water and the background consists of mountain and sky, the lightness and brightness of which, when contrasted with the dark "enclosures" of the frontal plane, imply an infinitely receding space.

These canons create a certain stability and predictability in Claude's landscapes, and coupled with his atmospheric, nearly magical light, transform these paintings into idylls. Claude's scenes are thus associated with a pastoral arcadia, and in their improvements and idealizations, they turn nature into art.

As a result, when narrative is injected into these representations, much of their drama is drained. The figures are small in comparison with the sweep of the land, and the formulaic landscape runs counter to the tension of the scene. The tale itself is subordinated to the poetry of nature, although here the figure of St. George is noticeable enough to imply that this is more than pure landscape.

FRENCH, GOBELINS

Don Quixote Consults the Enchanted Head at the House of Don Antonio

Ca. 1735
Tapestry: wool and silk
358.2 x 376 cm. (141 x 148 in.)
Gift of Elisha E. Hilliard
Acquisition no. 1945.349

Near the conclusion of Cervantes's epic tale, Don Quixote has a brush with the supernatural. In the house of Don Antonio, he and other guests are introduced to a magic marble head that will answer all questions truthfully. In response to Don Quixote's inquiry, the head prophesies, among other things, that Sancho Panza will receive a beating. It is this episode that has been woven into the tapestry illustrated here. Don Quixote bends down to listen, while Sancho Panza understandably starts in alarm.

This hanging is one of a large series of *Don Quixote* tapestries produced by the Gobelins workshops outside Paris. Between 1714 and 1794 nine sets of Don Quixote tapestries were made, based on the designs of Charles-Antoine Coypel. The Gobelins factory had been established in 1607. In 1662 it was taken over by the Crown, and during the next century some of France's most noted artists worked there. Charles Le Brun was among the first; he was followed by Coypel, Claude Audran, and François Boucher.

Don Quixote Consults the Enchanted Head was woven in 1735, after the Coypel cartoon and under the supervision of Audran. Audran's signature appears at the lower right, and all four corners show the monogram of Louis XV. The *Don Quixote* series is of particular note because it introduced *alentours*, a *trompe l'oeil* framing device of a richly garlanded border that reduces the main scene to a relatively small quadrant of the hanging. This border provided a standard format that could be repeated through a series, and since it could be executed by less skilled weavers, it proved to be a popular and economical innovation. The *alentour* seen here was designed by Belin de Fonteny in conjunction with the original Coypel cartoons in 1714. However, it is the central scene that commands our attention. The various characters strike the poses of the *Comédie Française*, and the elaborate interior looks like a small, intimate stage. Indeed, the *alentour* heightens the effect of artifice and theatricality, and in looking at this tableau, one eagerly anticipates the following scene.

64

A.L.G.

ST. PETERSBURG

The Finding of Moses

Ca. 1785
Tapestry: wool, silk, and silver
wrapped around a thread core
243.9 x 175.2 cm. (96 x 69 in.)
Gift of Elisha E. Hilliard
Acquisition no. 1947.443

Peter the Great's decision to wrench eighteenth-century Russia out of its medieval past and into the mainstream of European civilization had an impact on all aspects of life. Factories, shipyards, and even the entire city of St. Petersburg were rapidly developed after the example of Western European industry, art, and architecture in the age of the Baroque. Among Peter's many projects was the construction of a tapestry works in St. Petersburg in 1716. He took on this enterprise with characteristic large-scale ambition: in 1717 he applied to the renowned Gobelins factory in France for workmen, and a number of French (and possibly Flemish) artisans travelled to Russia to establish a workshop. By the 1760s a generation of Russian apprentices had been trained and the factory began a period of exuberant activity.

The tapestry reproduced here is typical of those produced during the reign of Catherine the Great (1762–96). It probably dates from about 1785, and was executed during the joint directorships of Count Audrey Shouvaloff and Prince Youssapoff (1783–90). The familiar Old Testament scene is represented in an antique mode; the Egyptian princess and her maid are dressed in the timeless drapery of the ancient Greeks. The composition is based on a painting in the Hermitage by the French classicist Eustache Le Sueur (1617–55), and his name appears at the top of the hanging. It was common practice then for the Russian weavers to copy the masterpieces in the Imperial collection; tapestries exist after Correggio, Guido Reni, and Boucher, as well as Russian artists.

There is another Russian tapestry in the Wadsworth Atheneum; its composition is based on Guercino's *St. Jerome*. These two pieces are among the very few examples of St. Petersburg tapestry to be found in public collections in America.

A.L.G.

CANALETTO

b. Venice, 1697
d. Venice, 1768

View of Venice, Piazza and Piazzetta San Marco

Ca. 1740–45
Oil on canvas
66 x 102.9 cm. (26 x 40 1/2 in.)
The Ella Gallup Sumner and
   Mary Catlin Sumner Collection
Acquisition no. 1947.2

Giovanni Antonio Canal, called Canaletto, was the Venetian master of the *veduta,* the "view" painting. Before the invention of photography, tourists who wished to recall their journeys purchased paintings as souvenirs. Akin to the picture postcard, the *vedute* were scenes of the most popular tourist attractions, executed in oil and often reproduced as etchings to be sold to a wider audience.

Because the *veduta* functions as a forerunner to souvenir photos, it is intriguing to note that to help record these scenes Canaletto employed mechanical aids, such as the *camera obscura,* which was actually a primitive form of the modern camera. Most likely, the use of this device accounts for the sometimes odd perspective and all-encompassing panorama of his images. This is particularly evident in the *View of Venice, Piazza and Piazzetta San Marco.* The focal point of the piece is the famous belltower of the Piazza San Marco at the center, with a plunging tunnel of space formed by the radically foreshortened facade of the Basilica of San Marco and the adjacent Doges' Palace on the left which funnel into a distant view of ships on the canal. To the right, the length of the piazza fans out, and taken as a whole, the scene has an elaborate inclusiveness, with many objects compressed into space—a characteristic of wide-angle photography.

Equally striking is the clarity of detail of the canvas. None of the complexity of the Venetian architecture is ignored, and amidst this grand setting is a careful depiction of the life of the square: the stalls of its marketplace, figures dressed in all manner of costumes and engaged in a variety of social interactions, and even playful small dogs. Canaletto, who also did set designs, saw Venetian life as pageantry, a kind of living theater. Like much of Canaletto's work, the scene is airy and fresh, with a luminosity that looks ahead to French Impressionism. It is believed that he may have worked, on occasion, out of doors.

Venice in general and the square of San Marco in particular were Canaletto's favorite subjects. Venice was as much of a tourist spot in the eighteenth century as it is now, and Canaletto had a clientele, especially in England, eager to own nearly anything he painted.

GIOVANNI PAOLO PANNINI

b. Piancenza, 1691/5
d. Rome, 1765/7

The Gallery of Cardinal Valenti Gonzaga

1749
Oil on canvas
198.1 x 268 cm. (78 x 105 ½ in.)
The Ella Gallup Sumner and
   Mary Catlin Sumner Collection
Acquisition no. 1948.478

Giovanni Paolo Pannini was one of several popular Italian eighteenth-century painters known as the *vedutisti* ("view painters"). Whereas Canaletto, another of the great *vedutisti*, was known for his Venetian scenes, Pannini recorded Rome. Providing painted and etched equivalents of today's picture postcard or souvenir snapshot, Pannini portrayed Rome's most popular tourist attractions. These were primarily the city's famous antique ruins, and Pannini's depictions satisfied not only the tourist's appetite for the scenic but also the vogue for the ancient world current among scholars, poets, artists, and intellectuals, as well as sightseers. Intriguingly, many of Pannini's scenes, despite their scrupulous detail and illusion of architectural accuracy, were compendiums of several sites or simply invented scenes. But for the tourist and the poet of the time, evoking the classical rather than duplicating it was what mattered.

Pannini also developed a reputation as a painter of art collections. In these works, he again provided tourists and scholars with souvenirs and documents of Rome. But in addition, he was actually chronicling the collecting mania then sweeping Italy and the rest of Europe. His paintings served as surrogates for those who aspired to or fantasized about possessing a great collection.

This is made clear in Pannini's *Gallery of Cardinal Valenti Gonzaga*. The painting is a veritable museum of great works, but there is some conjecture concerning the authenticity of this representation. First, the gallery may be sheer fabrication, and the collection itself is stocked with a few too many masterpieces. Although many of the paintings shown did belong to the Cardinal, some may be copies, and some of the works, such as the Raphael at the center, are elaborations of the original. Like his imaginary amalgamations of Roman ruins, Pannini's "picture gallery" may well personify the "ideal" collection rather than an existing one. Furthermore, this pictorial encyclopedia of the history of art is a technical tour de force, with its accomplished draftsmanship and magnificent space. The sense of collecting as a benevolent obsession is brilliantly suggested with the portrayal of recently unpacked purchases and dealers hawking more wares.

BERNHARD HEINRICH WEYE

b. Osnabrück, 1732
d. Augsburg, 1782

Centerpiece: Pergola with Serving Vessels

1757
Gilded silver
66 x 70.9 x 54.5 cm. (26 x 28 x
  21 1/2 in.)
J. J. Goodwin Fund
Acquisition no. 1950.437

With the ascent to the Imperial Hapsburg throne by Frederick II in 1740, Germany entered the gilded age of the Rococo. Frederick was a great Francophile and connoisseur of the arts; under his rule German taste was shaped by the example of the glittering courts of France. This remarkable and elaborate pergola was designed by Bernhard Heinrich Weye, one of the leading silversmiths of the time. It was made for the court of Augsburg in Bavaria, then a wealthy free-imperial city and a major center for silver and gold work.

This piece captures the essence of the fantastic and whimsical Rococo taste. The architecture echoes in miniature the great reception halls and intimate chambers of contemporary palaces. While its chief purpose was to astound and delight with its wealth of exuberant detail, it also served as a centerpiece for a banquet table. It has containers for condiments and is accompanied by several vessels, including a shaker, a teapot, and two covered bowls. It is likely that at least four more pots originally made up this set.

Function aside, it is the minute figures that attract our attention. Tucked into the arabesques of the trellis are trumpet-blowing and drumming cherubs, and in the center are a number of musicians. These are dressed in the quaint *style rustique* made popular by Marie Antoinette. Even their music can be read—the notes of what was probably a local song. In its sophisticated and witty charm, this centerpiece preserves the spirit of the Rococo court in which etiquette, ceremony, and luxury reigned supreme.

A.L.G.

JEAN-BAPTISTE GREUZE

b. Tournus, 1725
d. Paris, 1805

Indolence

1756–57
Oil on canvas
64.8 x 50 cm. (25 1/2 x 19 11/16 in.)
The Ella Gallup Sumner and
    Mary Catlin Sumner Collection
Acquisition no. 1934.11

In the art of Jean-Baptiste Greuze, sentiment is coupled with didacticism to deliver moral messages designed to appeal to the middle class. In an age when the instructions of Rousseau and Diderot were popular, Greuze tried to provide visual counterparts to their teachings. In this, he was influenced by two key artistic traditions: Dutch and Flemish art and Italian and French classicism. From Dutch and Flemish art, he acquired an approach to genre. From the Italian and French, he borrowed figural types that carry the weight of Renaissance and classical ideals.

Indolence is a typical example of Greuze's pious style. A bulky figure, she leans listlessly, surrounded by the mess produced by her character flaw. Unwashed dishes clutter the floor, basins spill their potentially cleansing contents, clothes are dishevelled and tattered. There is no relief from this disarray; the tipping figure is echoed by a wine jug askew (is a connection implied between indolence and inebriation?). The woman is so lethargic that she is unable to complete the simple task of putting on both shoes.

Despite its sentimentalism, there is much to appreciate in *Indolence*. The heavy figure possesses a dormant power, not unlike some of Michelangelo's figures. Texture is confidently rendered throughout, from the softness of clothes to the roughness of cracked pottery and decaying walls. Earth tones surround the pink and creamy white figure, who seems to exude a slow glow. Exhibited at the Salon in Paris in 1757, *Indolence* was a popular piece. Its popularity endures, for it was the centerpiece of a major retrospective of Greuze's art organized in 1977 at the Atheneum.

75

CARLE VANLOO

b. Nice, 1705
d. Paris, 1765

The Offering to Love

1761
Oil on canvas
160.5 x 98.8 cm. (63 3/16 x 38 7/8 in.)
The Ella Gallup Sumner and
    Mary Catlin Sumner Collection
Acquisition no. 1979.186

Carle Vanloo was one of the most famous artists of his time, though today his reputation is no longer so stellar. Part of an artistic family renowned in France for generations, Vanloo shuttled between France and Italy during his career. Although he did a number of important religious altarpieces, he is best known for his scenes combining elements of genre and mythology designed to evoke the Arcadian and the antique.

Vanloo's _The Offering to Love_ is typical of the preoccupation with the amorous during the age of the Rococo. After the death of Louis XIV, the aristocracy who had gathered around him at Versailles, returned to Paris. Previously curtailed by Louis from exercising their desire for extreme luxury, yet infected by the Sun King's own ostentation, the nobility, freed from the fetters of the court of Versailles, demonstrated their liberation with a vengeance. They became France's great consuming class, and their taste ran to the sensual, delightful, exotic, and frivolous. Thus, amorous scenes from mythology and games of courtly love, rather than ponderous subjects from history and religion, became the popular motifs of Rococo art.

The Offering to Love typifies this spirit of antique and romantic subjects. Figures clad in classical costumes (also a popular fashion of the day) come to place garlands at the foot of a statue of Amor (based on an actual sculpture by Falconet). The impish grin of Amor personifies the sweet and sometimes bittersweet effects of his powers. The style, too, is Rococo in its muted coloration, dominated by a pastel blue-green background against which are located figures and statues of predominantly gold, beige, and cream. Furthermore, there is a looseness of brushstrokes and a classicized fullness to the figures that illustrate the Rococo's continuation of certain Baroque techniques.

CHINESE

Wall Fountain and Basin

Qing dynasty, Kang Xi period,
  1680–1710
Porcelain with pewter faucet
Fountain: 45.8 cm. high (18 in.)
Basin: 42 cm. high (16 1/2 in.)
Gift of Samuel P. Avery
Acquisition nos. 1920.690–691

Private traders began to import Chinese porcelains to the West in the first years of the seventeenth century. At first these wares were considered secondary in value to the stores of spice and tea which were carried on the same ships. Soon, however, the market for these delicate and exotic works of art escalated, and by the close of the century Chinese porcelain could be found throughout Europe, in every conceivable form. Accordingly, the Chinese artisans adapted their patterns to accomodate Western demands, and commercial trade enterprises like the East India Company began to handle a great volume of wares. An inventory of 1703, recording the London sale of pieces brought back from the Chinese port of Amoy by the *Dashwood*, lists 1,370 chocolate cups, 380 dishes, 46 painted men, 144 parrots, 645 basins, 14 wall flower pots, 4 suckling bottles, 231 patch boxes, 26 Sancta Marias, 7 pulpits, 90 pipes, and over 3,000 other items.

This matched pair must have arrived in a similar shipment. They were made during the reign of the Emperor Kang Xi, who had particularly promoted the manufacture and sale of porcelain for export. The fountain and basin must have been made specifically for the European market, for their form and function are alien to Oriental fashion. However, the translucent *famille verte* glazes, brilliant colors, and sophisticated decoration are all uniquely Chinese. Multicolored glazes, such as those seen here, had been introduced in the late seventeenth century, and were soon favored over the traditional blue and white glaze of the Ming dynasty. The surface of the glaze is minutely nuanced, with the deep grey shades slightly raised and the border pattern lightly incised. The upended flora and fauna of the sea appear to be swept along by an unseen current. Although the technique of firing porcelain was successfully copied in Germany after 1709, Occidental artists never assimilated this kind of graceful manipulation of perspective and pattern, illusion and design.

A.L.G.

GERMAN

Meissen Vase and Beakers

Ca. 1722–30
Hard-paste porcelain
Vase: 63.5 cm. high (25 in.)
Beakers: 41.3 cm. high (16 1/4 in.)
Gift of J. Pierpont Morgan
Acquisition nos. 1917.1186–1190

As the market for Chinese porcelains expanded, European craftsmen undertook numerous projects in an attempt to copy this fine, light, and resilient pottery. It was only after decades of experimentation that a successful formula for "true" hard-paste porcelain was discovered in 1709 by Johann Friedrich Böttger in Dresden. Since porcelain then commanded fantastically high prices, Böttger received immediate support from the Elector of Saxony, Augustus the Strong, who founded the Royal Saxon Porcelain Factory in 1710 in Meissen. Böttger was named head of the factory, and he and his assistants worked in virtual isolation (in order to protect the secret of the formula) over the next nine years, perfecting and refining the medium, firing process, and glazes.

By the 1720s, Böttger's followers were able to produce a large body of porcelain wares. Johann Gregor Höroldt became chief painter at Meissen in 1720, and he introduced the brilliantly polychromed objects glazed in the "Chinese" style. Here we have three of a five-piece set that dates from this initial period of the Meissen factory. Surface bubbles, cracks, and warps suggest that these were created during the first ambitious and experimental stage of production. The shapes of the beakers and vase were dictated by Chinese examples, and the boldly applied glazes show a knowledge of Oriental design and composition.

While these pieces may appear crude when compared to later Meissen works, they attest to the triumphant first years of European porcelain. They were meant to be displayed together, as an ornamental garniture on top of a cabinet or chimney-piece. They are marked with Augustus's insignia "A.R." and were made either for his personal use or as a royal gift.

A.L.G.

VINCENNES

Basket of Flowers

1749–53
Soft-paste porcelain with wire details
61 cm. high (24 in.)
Gift of J. Pierpont Morgan
Acquisition no. 1917.1234

This basket of flowers, meant to serve as a centerpiece, was probably made at the royal factory in Vincennes in the middle of the eighteenth century, at the height of the Rococo. The painter François Boucher, a favorite of Madame de Pompadour, had established in the French court a taste for the whimsical and colorful. All the decorative arts of the period reflect this preference, none better than the masterly porcelains of St.-Cloud, Vincennes, and later, Sèvres.

The factory at Vincennes was established in 1738, and its primary aim was to rival the porcelains of the Saxon factory in Meissen. However, once the technical difficulties were mastered, Vincennes developed its own distinctive style characterized by an emphasis on floral patterns. The first full floral bouquet was designed for the Queen of France in 1748. Mounted on a gilt-bronze base, it contains a profusion of flowers similar to the one seen here, and was hailed by French contemporaries as "surpassing Meissen." The admiration accorded this piece prompted further bouquets, and records show that forty-six girls were employed exclusively for the painting and assembling of flower arrangements, mounting them on wire stems embellished with metal leaves.

The preferred medium for this kind of work was a malleable soft-paste porcelain. While it lacked the resilience of true porcelain, and was too fragile for utilitarian purposes, it was admired for its exceptional delicacy. In general, soft-paste porcelain remained in use for such work in France until the end of the eighteenth century.

The factory at Vincennes was moved to Sèvres in 1756 due to financial difficulties. Sèvres porcelain is now world famous; however, that of Vincennes remains peerless in its inventiveness, freshness, and vitality.

A.L.G.

STAFFORDSHIRE

Three Teapots

1750–70
Salt-glazed stoneware
11.5 cm. high each (4 1/2 in.)
Gift of J. Pierpont Morgan
Acquisition nos. 1917.372, 374, 377

England is proverbially a nation of tea drinkers. Therefore it is not surprising to discover in English pottery a remarkable variety of vessels for the beverage that "cheers but does not inebriate." After tea was commercially introduced into England in 1657 (when it was billed as a form of medicine), the English rapidly invented their own form of tea ceremony. Potters throughout the environs of London and the west of England immediately rose to the occasion.

Numerous small factories sprang up in the Staffordshire district in the eighteenth century, and it was here that some of the most popular tea services, as well as other decorative pieces, were made. These factories, while built on a far smaller scale than the royal ones of Meissen and Sèvres, managed to produce wares not only for domestic use, but also for export to the continent and America. Salt-glaze stoneware, a form of porcelain, was favored. Like porcelain, stoneware can be highly fired, which makes it delicate and translucent. Although derived from continental stoneware, the hard saline glazes are an English characteristic.

Around 1740, color was introduced in the Staffordshire pieces, and the blue-tinted teapots illustrated here are examples of a unique form of underglaze known as "Littler blue," invented by William Littler. Instead of being painted on, the pigment was mixed with the stoneware clay before the initial firing. Later the decoration was added over this tinted ground. The third pot is graced by a portrait of Frederick III, King of Prussia. This was undoubtedly glazed to commemorate a state occasion, and reminds us of the popular modern pots and cups that are mass-produced to celebrate every English coronation and royal wedding. All three pots display the rustic "crabstock" handles that came into fashion after 1750.

A.L.G.

JOSEPH WRIGHT OF DERBY

b. Derby, 1734
d. Derby, 1797

The Old Man and Death

Ca. 1774
Oil on canvas
101.6 x 127.2 cm. (40 x 50 $^1/_{16}$ in.)
The Ella Gallup Sumner and
   Mary Catlin Sumner Collection
Acquisition no. 1953.15

As his name implies, Joseph Wright spent most of his life in Derby, in the Midlands region of England, an area that became one of the first centers of the Industrial Revolution. Wright, who was fascinated by science and mechanics as a child, put this interest to use by making industry and technology among the key themes of his art. His patrons, logically, included new wealthy industrialists, as well as inventors, scientists, and intellectuals.

Like an experimenting scientist, Wright set up challenges in his art that often required the use of great skill and acute powers of observation. One of his particular tasks was the depiction of light, and throughout his career Wright investigated artificial light (often seen through intervening objects), moonlight, all conditions of daylight, fireworks, firelight, and the glow of spewing volcanic ash. His preoccupation with science, with its orderly methods and belief in verifiable truths, places him within the eighteenth-century tradition of the Enlightenment.

However, like many eighteenth-century artists, Wright had his Romantic side. His *Old Man and Death*, depicting the gruesomeness of mortality rather than the wonders of science, is an example of this Romanticism. Based on an Aesop's fable, the painting portrays an old man so burdened by the hardships of life that he drops his bundles of sticks and summons death for relief. But the aged man has a change of heart and succeeds in warding off death's calling. Despite the "Gothick" quality of the scene, with its image of approaching death, the terror of the old worker, and the overgrown ruins described by crusty areas of paint, Wright still scrupulously records the condition of bright daylight and portrays the skeleton with the accuracy of an anatomist.

FRANCISCO JOSÉ DE GOYA

b. Fuente de Todos, Spain, 1746
d. Bordeaux, 1828

Gossiping Women

Ca. 1787–91
Oil on canvas
58.9 x 145.4 cm. (23 3/16 x 57 1/4 in.)
The Ella Gallup Sumner and
 Mary Catlin Sumner Collection
Acquisition no. 1929.4

One of the key characteristics of the work of the great Spanish artist Francisco de Goya is its concern with the powers of reason. Goya presents a world in which reason creates order or the lack of reason produces chaos. Most often in his work, irrationality prevails and chaos wins out. Thus he chronicles man's weaknesses, from his mildest follies and foibles to his most gross injustices and horrors.

Among Goya's most famous pieces are the etchings called *The Disasters of War* and the trenchant portraits of Spanish royalty done when he was court painter. A work such as *Gossiping Women*, from the 1790s, indicates another area of Goya's art. In theme, this piece falls midway between his early genre scenes and his later *Caprichos*—the title of a sometimes harshly incisive series on such human disorders as greed, superstition, violence, cruelty, and ignorance. *Gossiping Women* initially recalls the Rococo genre tradition of the depiction of games, love, leisure, and entertainment. But here all is not lightheartedness and frivolity: the sinister potential of gossip is implied in the eager, almost hungry expressions of the women as they exchange forbidden information. Thus, what seems to be an innocent genre scene, when probed more profoundly, reveals a nascent evil later made explicit in the *Caprichos*.

Stylistically, the piece can be placed within a Rococo and Romantic tradition, and it is especially reminiscent of Tiepolo's art. Goya wields a wide brush and produces fetching juxtapositions of colors: reds are set against blues; greens against lavenders and russets; and variously tinged whites against golds. It is the contrasts, however, between areas of light and dark that are paramount. Within the parenthesis of a dark landscape, a central, highlighted body of a woman looms, and the folds of her skirt, which covers her buttocks, project toward the viewer's space. Located in a thin plane of dark is a second woman, who in turn is backlit by a pale blue and slate sky. The transition from light to dark, from the first woman to the second, suggests the transmission of gossip from the one who knows (in light) but whose secret remains intact (because she keeps her back to us), to the darker, uninformed friend.

JEAN AUGUSTE DOMINIQUE INGRES

b. Montauban, 1780
d. Paris, 1867

Ferdinand Philippe, Duc d'Orleans

1844
Oil on canvas
73 x 60.2 cm. (28 3/4 x 23 11/16 in.)
The Ella Gallup Sumner and
     Mary Catlin Sumner Collection
Acquisition no. 1953.95

In the early and mid-nineteenth century in France, a battle was waged between two artistic camps: Neoclassicism and Romanticism, whose respective generals were Jean Auguste Dominique Ingres and Eugène Delacroix. Ingres, a follower of Jacques Louis David, began his career as a painter of scenes from Roman history. Like most devotees of classicism, Ingres sought to depict the ideal rather than the real. But one of the dangers, or perhaps rewards, of this pursuit is that in striving for perfection, one departs further and further from the natural and grows close to the artificial and abstract. Herein lies the originality of Ingres's art. In its combination of microscopic observation, polished surfaces, icy, clear colorism, and linearity bordering on abstraction, his art achieves a unique position that hovers between the obsessively accurate and the totally artificial. However, his personal obsession with exoticism often brought his art close to the Romantic school.

In addition to classical themes, Ingres's repertoire included religion, allegory, mythology, history, and portraiture. His chilly style served him well in portraying the French aristocracy. The painting of *Ferdinand Philippe, Duc d'Orleans* in the Wadsworth Atheneum is an abbreviated version of the same figure done in a three-quarter-length pose around 1842–43. Ferdinand Philippe, who died in 1842, was Louis Philippe's eldest son. The queen commissioned this portrait head in 1844, to be given to the late Prince Ferdinand's preceptor, Guérard.

The portrait possesses the typical hauteur of Ingres's subjects. The elongated head and neck emphasize aloofness, and the restraint and rigidity of the physiognomy repel rather than reveal. The stiffness and hermeticism of the figure derive, in part, from Ingres's study of the Italian Mannerist Bronzino, who similarly invested his portraits with coolness and reserve.

91

EUGENE DELACROIX

b. Charenton-Saint-Maurire, 1798
d. Paris, 1863

Turkish Women Bathing

1854
Oil on canvas
92.1 x 77.5 cm. (36 1/4 x 30 1/2 in.)
The Ella Gallup Sumner and
  Mary Catlin Sumner Collection
Acquisition no. 1952.300

In the debate between Neoclassical and Romantic art in France in the nineteenth century, Eugène Delacroix was cast as the leading proponent of Romanticism. As a Romantic, Delacroix popularized new sources for subject matter in art, such as the Medieval and non-Western worlds, and the works of Shakespeare, Byron, and Scott. Paintings no longer needed to be didactic and edifying: indeed, the exotic, the mysterious, even the gruesome became worthy themes. Stylistically, Romanticism implied painterliness, in which brushstroke and color, rather than line, formed the underpinnings of the work. Favoring the Baroque over the Renaissance, Romantic artists adopted diagonal thrusts into space and curvilinear movements on the canvas surface as their primary compositional arrangements, instead of mathematically precise, one-point perspective systems of parallel planes and geometric configurations.

Delacroix expressed the Romantic sensibility best in certain canvases that combined a number of the aforementioned interests. For example, his *Massacre at Chios*, of 1824, and his *Death of Sardanapalus*, of 1827–28, deal with exotic themes highlighting acts of heroism and horror. But his most famous painting, *Liberty Leading the People*, of 1832, treats the contemporary subject of the 1832 Revolution. This work also demonstrates that Delacroix, despite his Romantic affiliation, often raided antiquity and the Renaissance for pictorial models. The work has the allegorical trappings of a typical Neoclassical piece, although it is not couched in terms of classical philosophy, but rather in the framework of the actual horrors of the war.

Color, always a motivating force in Delacroix's art, became the major preoccupation of his most mature works. *Turkish Women Bathing* is one such late piece in which hue dominates. The painting is lush with the blue-green tones of water, foliage, and sky, punctuated by the golden, glowing, creamy flesh tones of women bathing and lounging. A trip to Morocco in 1832 intensified Delacroix's concern for color, and here the jewellike tones, as well as the exotic subject, are drawn from studies and memories of his journey. Paint is applied fairly broadly, and space recedes in diagonal slices, from the two figures in the left foreground, to the stream and its swimmer, and finally to the women on the far bank. Sensuality pervades the scene: we are treated not simply to a view of disporting nudes, whose beauty is akin to the swans of the water, but are also witness to the scene voyeuristically, with the protective, arching bows of the trees implying a glimpse into a private world.

93

EDGAR DEGAS

b. Paris, 1834
d. Paris, 1917

Double Portrait—The Cousins of the Painter

Ca. 1865
Oil on canvas
57 x 70 cm. (22 7/16 x 27 9/16 in.)
The Ella Gallup Sumner and
   Mary Catlin Sumner Collection
Acquisition no. 1934.36

Though he was close to several of the Impressionists and exhibited in most of the major exhibitions of the movement, Edgar Degas was a highly individual artist whose approach, outlook, and technique differed measurably from that of mainstream Impressionism. Degas's obsession was modern life: his art is an inquiry into developing metropolitan society in all of its facets, from its visual rhythms to its manners and psychology. True, the Impressionists were also preoccupied by the modern world and the activities of its emerging middle class, and frequently their art evokes the psychology of modern society, especially its potential alienation and dehumanization. But for the most part, mainstream Impressionism was an art of pure perception, an attempt to present the world optically, not conceptually or psychologically. Degas's curiosity penetrated deeper than visual appearance, deeper than the studies of light, atmosphere, climate, and time of day that occupied the Impressionists. The result was an art of great intelligence, stylistically inspired by sources as diverse as Ingres, Delacroix, Japanese woodcuts, and, perhaps, photography, and which shared the avant-garde disdain for the ingratiating and the superficial. His art suggests, perhaps, that Impressionism be divided into two branches: one, purely perceptual depictions of street scenes and landscapes; the other, more figurative works, focusing on the kinetics and psychology of contemporary society.

Degas's mastery at probing personality is felt most strikingly in his portraits. Members of his family and relatives frequently sat for him; here his Italian cousins Camille and Hélène Montejasi-Cicerale are the subjects of this *Double Portrait*. Placed against an indeterminate, splotchily brushed earth- and rust-toned background, the two sisters, similarly dressed and obviously close in resemblance, assert their individuality in their respective poses. Degas dramatically transforms this dual portrait into a presentation of differing personalities: one sister is direct, sober and confrontational; the other, by turning away, appears pensive, melancholy, shy, less communicative. In style and composition, Degas focuses all attention on the heads of the figures. The loosely brushed background and the dark, thinly painted clothing are cursorily descriptive passages, while the faces are carefully and smoothly modelled with a clarity suggestive of the work of Ingres and Northern Renaissance art. But even this sense of finish is not identical in the two faces: that of the more direct sister is firmly polished, and the oblique girl's face is softer, muted, almost fading.

95

PIERRE AUGUSTE RENOIR

b. Limoges, 1841
d. Cagnes, 1919

***Monet Painting in His Garden at
Argenteuil***

1873
Oil on canvas
50.2 x 106.7 cm. (19¾ x 42 in.)
Bequest of Anne Parrish Titzell
Acquisition no. 1957.614

96

Auguste Renoir's *Monet Painting in his Garden at Argenteuil* is a revealing document of the vision and procedures of the French Impressionists. We see Monet with his easel set up out of doors, an approach called *plein-air* painting. The goal of the Impressionists was to record the visual world as the eye perceived it, not as the mind conceived it. In working out of doors, they were particularly attuned to the qualities of light; and they understood that light, as determined by weather, season, and time of day, often seems to dissolve the solidity of objects and to cast colored shadows on neighboring objects. The Impressionists also rejected the notion that reality was absolute; instead, they attempted to seize the qualities of specific, individual moments. What results is a fresh, light-filled canvas, with many paint strokes visible. Objects have lost their bulk and the quick touch of the artist's brush evokes an instantaneous condition.

CLAUDE MONET

b. Paris, 1840
d. Giverny, 1926

Beach at Trouville

1872
Oil on canvas
52.1 x 59.1 cm. (20 1/2 x 23 1/4 in.)
The Ella Gallup Sumner and
   Mary Catlin Sumner Collection
Acquisition no. 1948.116

While we often associate Impressionism with landscape, it is, in some respects, a cosmopolitan art. City scenes figure prominently among Impressionist canvases, and rural motifs are generally the resorts accessible by trains and frequented by the Parisian middle class. *Beach at Trouville* is precisely one such seaside spot, and Monet records a typical moment of vacationers strolling along the shore. The work is light-filled and fresh, with visible paint strokes, indicating Monet's attempt to capture fleeting atmospheric conditions. Probably painted out of doors and in direct contact with the scene, *Beach at Trouville* has a brightness and briskness that were normally subdued in traditional art. Like Renoir and the other Impressionists, Monet's aim was to record pure visual perception. It was this radical emphasis on vision that provoked such controversy when Impressionist painting was first exhibited in a group show in Paris in 1874. Although Impressionist painting often concentrated on subjects of middle-class leisure and entertainment, it was the bourgeoisie who were most shocked by this unidealized art that failed to deal with heroic, weighty subjects.

PAUL CEZANNE

b. Aix-en-Provence, 1839
d. Aix-en-Provence, 1906

Portrait of a Child

Ca. 1883–84
Oil on canvas
27.9 x 32.1 cm. (11 x 12 5/8 in.)
The Ella Gallup Sumner and Mary
  Catlin Sumner Collection
Acquisition no. 1968.195

The art of Paul Cézanne has had a profound effect on the course of modern art. Cézanne's ability to achieve a "harmony parallel to nature," in which patches of paint simultaneously function as units of construction and as indicators of naturalistic objects, offered a lesson on art that contemporary painters are still trying to fathom.

Cézanne arrived at his mature style after several decades of diverse work. In the 1860s, he painted literary, religious, and fantasy scenes, applying thick slabs of paint with a palette knife. Products of his imagination, these often violent subjects were subdued considerably in the 1870s, when he worked with the Impressionist painter Camille Pissarro. Pissarro, who functioned as something of a father figure to Cézanne, encouraged the younger artist to accept nature rather than his turbulent fabrications as his guide in art. Pissarro's Impressionist working methods were also influential: Cézanne lightened and brightened his palette, began applying paint in thinner blocks, and became increasingly interested in conditions of light and atmosphere.

This immersion in French Impressionism became the foundation of his later work. But rather than dissolving form into an atmospheric flicker of light, Cézanne took the emancipated brush and color of Impressionism and developed a unique "patch" stroke which created formal harmony on the canvas surface while rendering the objects of nature (even though conventional modelling and the contrasts of light and shade were eliminated). In this respect, Cézanne operates as a painter-phenomenologist, reorganizing perceptions through a filter of tone, line, color, and form.

His *Portrait of a Child*, probably dating from about 1883, is a somewhat modest, perhaps unfinished work, but in it we can still recognize Cézanne's ability to assert formal autonomy and at the same time offer a sensitive portrayal of a young boy. Family members were often his models, and here Cézanne most likely has selected his son as his subject.

HENRI DE TOULOUSE-LAUTREC

b. Albi, 1864
d. Malromé Castle, Gironde, 1901

Jane Avril Leaving the Moulin Rouge

1892
Essence on cardboard
84.5 x 63.5 cm. (33 1/4 x 25 in.)
Bequest of George A. Gay
Acquisition no. 1941.163

Jane Avril Leaving the Moulin Rouge offers some of the salient characteristics of Henri de Toulouse-Lautrec's art. Lautrec selects a moment when this well-known performer is offstage, in order to capture her essence rather than her facade. The artist, in the French tradition of the *flâneur*, noticeable also in the work of Daumier, Degas, and Manet, was a keen observer of life. He believed that the truth of individuals is best exposed when they are caught unawares, with their defenses down. Thus, we are witness to the famous French dancer, Jane Avril, as she leaves her work, alone, introspective, and devoid of her vibrant energy.

The subject of popular dance and dance halls was one of a class of themes preferred by Lautrec which included cafes, brothels, and the circus. Partly as a result of his own physical deformity, he became a member of the Parisian demimonde and a devotée of its seamy, decadent dives and haunts. His milieu was Montmartre, home of the Parisian avant garde and a center of creativity and eccentricity—not unlike other later bohemian locales such as Greenwich Village and SoHo.

Because he was as fascinated by kinetics and rhythm as he was by psyche and personality, Lautrec also did numerous portraits of Jane Avril dancing. He designed posters for many of the cafes at which famous dancers performed. In his poster work, he learned the value of simplifying form into bold, arresting patterns intended to captivate the passerby. In *Jane Avril Leaving the Moulin Rouge* he uses gouache, and locks the form of Jane Avril into a tight pattern of space. Her face, chalky, jaundiced, and pinched, with a thin gash of red for lips, is encased in a firmly contoured area of streaks of blues, violets, and occasional greens, which define her apparel. Intriguingly, Lautrec de-emphasizes any sense of anatomy beneath her clothing: her performance has taken its toll—she is sapped of energy, and her expressive limbs and torso, so essential to the dancer, appear inconsequential. Her form stands in sharp contrast to a tan cardboard ground and a wall flecked with specks and slashes of yellow. Space is flattened by a bird's-eye viewpoint, and a syncopation of forms emerges as a result of secondary blue shapes alternating with the yellow-tan zones surrounding Jane Avril.

PAUL GAUGUIN

b. Paris, 1848
d. Tahiti, 1903

Nirvana: Portrait of Meyer de Haan

Ca. 1890
Oil thinned with turpentine on linen
20.3 x 29.2 cm. (8 x 11 ½ in.)
The Ella Gallup Sumner and Mary
 Catlin Sumner Collection
Acquisition no. 1943.445

The reputation of Paul Gauguin has achieved almost mythic proportions, and it functions as a paradigm for the notion of the avant-garde artist. A stockbroker and family man, he severed his commercial and familial ties at the age of thirty-five and devoted himself completely to a career in art. Initially working in an Impressionist manner, Gauguin eventually forged a distinctive style that was to have great impact in the art world. This was Synthetism, in which objects, when translated into paint, were simplified, purged of modelling, flattened, heavily silhouetted, and composed of nearly unmodulated hues, all arranged in harmonious fashion on the canvas. This style was symptomatic of Gauguin's desire to strip art of inessentials, and in this pursuit, he combed the history of art and the contemporary world for like-minded creations. His belief in the purity, innocence, and consequent power of such art, coupled with his disgust for sophisticated, intellectualized, cosmopolitan life (a sentiment common among late nineteenth-century antimaterialists), resulted in his travelling to locales where the unadulterated life could be found.

One region was nearby: the province of Brittany in northern France, where peasants continued to live in a manner that seemed untouched by the advances of civilization. His most famous destination was Tahiti (one of several exotic lands that he visited), where Gauguin studied native folk art, lived among its people, and spent the last years of his life.

Nirvana: Portrait of Meyer de Haan was done in Brittany in 1890. The Dutchman Jacob Meyer de Haan was associated with a colony of artists gathered around Gauguin in Brittany, where painters worked in a "Synthetist" manner. Since the style of this art stressed suggestion and evocation over reproduction and representation, it was claimed by the current Symbolist movement as the pictorial branch of their sensibility. In this painting, Gauguin demonstrates the style with deflated space, reduced modelling, and clearly outlined color shapes. Paint is applied with a visible stroke—a legacy of Impressionism. Furthermore, the hunchback De Haan is surrounded by nude figures, and one wonders whether the title *Nirvana* refers to the realm of the spirit, suggested by the meditative painter, or the realm of the flesh, suggested by the serpent he holds in his hand (an image also used in Gauguin's *Self-Portrait with Halo*), which may be a reference to sin or temptation. That sin and temptation might be the key theme is evident in De Haan's fox-like appearance (originally modelled after a Peruvian mummy from an ethnological museum), an image that crops up as a symbol of licentiousness in other Gauguin paintings, while the scene behind De Haan may represent the temptation and fall of Eve. (See Wayne Anderson, *The Burlington Magazine*, vol. 109, p. 239 f.)

WILLIAM HOLMAN HUNT

b. London, 1827
d. London, 1910

The Lady of Shalott

Ca. 1886–1905
Oil on canvas
188 x 146 cm. (74 x 57 ½ in.)
The Ella Gallup Sumner and
    Mary Catlin Sumner Collection
Acquisition no. 1961.470

The Pre-Raphaelite Brotherhood, founded in England in 1848, attempted to restore purity and honesty to art, based upon the style and subjects of work done before the time of Raphael. Among the main motivations behind such art were a disgust for the dehumanization caused by the Industrial Revolution and for the repression of man's true instincts, especially sexual ones, during the Victorian age. Since a great deal of their art was moralistic and much of it was based on themes borrowed from poetry and literature, especially from Medieval themes, the Pre-Raphaelites adopted a highly graphic and carefully detailed style which they felt could best communicate their messages. Curiously, this fascination with accuracy often produced an intensity that made their subjects appear artificial and dreamlike, but this sensibility was often appropriate to the romantic, exotic, and rarefied themes of much of their work.

William Holman Hunt was one of the initial founders of the Pre-Raphaelite Brotherhood and, like the rest of his comrades, was in his early twenties when the movement was established. Hunt was perhaps the most literary and didactic of the group, and Shakespeare, Dickens, Keats, and the Bible were among his favorite sources. *The Lady of Shalott* is derived from the famous poem by Alfred, Lord Tennyson; it is an Arthurian tale of a Lady forbidden by an enchantment to look out her window. Shown the world instead through a mirror, she spends her days weaving the mirror's reflection, until the sight of Lancelot riding past tempts her to look out the window. The weaving thereupon snaps, and her tragic fate is fulfilled.

Hunt did several studies for this piece, including an illustration for an 1857 edition of the poet's work. As is often the case in Hunt's art, the theme is so overloaded with symbols and details that he succeeds in clouding the story rather than clarifying it. Even Tennyson was unsatisfied with it, to which Hunt retorted: "May I not urge that I had only half a page on which to convey the impression of weird fate, whereas you use about fifteen pages to give expression to the complete idea." Despite the problems that arise from Hunt's efforts to distill fifteen pages of text into one painting, *The Lady of Shalott* remains an astonishing work in its myriad images, colors, textures, and light effects. Its complexity and hyperrealism, reminiscent of that of Jan van Eyck, are a technical tour de force. Hunt uses a highly linear method, not only to describe the Lady's actual weaving, but also to suggest the sense of her entanglement in fate and the labyrinthine complications of the story itself.

LEON BAKST

b. St. Petersburg, 1868
d. Paris, 1924

*Costume Design for Nijinsky in
"L'Après-Midi d'un Faune"*

1912
Watercolor
39.1 x 26.7 cm. (15 3/8 x 10 1/2 in.)
The Ella Gallup Sumner and
    Mary Catlin Sumner Collection
Acquisition no. 1935.37

One of the great joys of the Wadsworth Atheneum is the Serge Lifar Collection of ballet, set, and costume designs. Lifar was a leading member of the famous Serge Diaghilev Ballet Russe, and his collection includes designs by Georges Rouault, Giorgio de Chirico, Pavel Tchelitchew, Jean Cocteau, Pablo Picasso, Alexandre Benois, and Léon Bakst.

Scandal and controversy accompanied many of the radical ballets performed by Diaghilev's company. *L'Après-Midi d'un Faune* was no exception. Léon Bakst designed the sets for this performance, but his costume for the Faun, played by the great Vaslav Nijinsky, was particularly shocking. Nijinsky was clad in the tightest of leotards dotted with huge dark ellipses, which resembled the spots on an animal. Further provocation was provided by a bunch of grapes covering his genitals. While such a costume hardly strikes us as alarming today, its brevity and sheerness were most unusual at the time. In fact, Diaghilev led the revolution toward greater sensuality and explicitness in ballet.

Premiering in Paris in 1912, *L'Après-Midi d'un Faune*, choreographed to Debussy's musical interpretation of the Mallarmé poem, was a *succès de scandale*. In the spirit of Bakst's designs, which also included nymphs clad only in gauzy tunics, Nijinsky gave a performance now legendary for its eroticism. As the Faun, he woos a nymph, who in evading the Faun's advance, drops her scarf. Nijinsky proceeded to kiss, caress, and simulate lovemaking to this surrogate, enraging most of his audience, though delighting some.

Bakst's watercolor shows Nijinsky in his notorious costume clutching a bunch of grapes and their leaves. Around him swirls a dazzling, sinuous blue form (the scarf of the nymph), decorated with an organic cornucopia motif common to Art Nouveau, which in this case may suggest fertility.

107

HENRI MATISSE

b. Cateau-Cambrésis, 1869
d. Nice-Cimiez, 1954

Woman with a Plumed Hat

1918
Oil on canvas
44.4 x 36.9 cm. (17 1/2 x 14 1/2 in.)
The Ella Gallup Sumner and
   Mary Catlin Sumner Collection
Acquisition no. 1969.1

In 1905, the critic Louis Vauxcelles (who is also credited with coining the term "Cubism"), in a review of a show at the Salon d'Automne in Paris, described a group of painters as *Fauves* or "wild beasts," and that label soon denominated an art movement. What must have struck Vauxcelles (who was not unsympathetic to this art) as "wild" and "beastly" was the stridency of color, the loose and expressive application of paint, and the dynamic sense of design of these works. Among those exhibiting was the thirty-six-year-old artist Henri Matisse.

The association of Matisse with Fauvism was somewhat ironic in that the movement was perceived as youth-oriented, anarchistic, and rebellious, and Matisse was mature and somewhat conservative in temperament. It is also ironic that his paintings should have appeared so savagely stimulating since Matisse's goal in art seemed contrary to this spirit: "What I dream of is an art of balance, of purity, of serenity, devoid of troubling or depressing subject matter, an art which might be . . . like an appeasing influence, like a mental soother, something like a good armchair in which to rest from physical fatigue." Much of Matisse's art aspires to that condition in its simplification, harmony, and order and in its pleasant presentation of themes of still life, landscape, portraiture, and figural groups in tranquil or arcadian settings.

Modest in size, *Woman with a Plumed Hat* is a portrait of Matisse's daughter Marguerite. Done in the late 1910s, when many artists were moving toward a more muted style, the painting lacks the stunning colors characteristic of Matisse's most exciting art. Many of his works from this period appear tranquil and subdued; they seem to reflect both a sense of relief at the approaching end of the war and a sobriety in response to its devastating events. Matisse's move to Nice, where *Woman with a Plumed Hat* may have been painted, and where he had contact with Pierre Bonnard and Auguste Renoir, also tempered his art, and at this time he executed a quiet series of lone female figures in interior settings.

This particular piece offers subtle pleasures in a harmony of blues, greens, and greys, lightly accented by oranges, violets, and off-whites. Though there is some modelling to the figure, the space of the work is primarily flat. There is also an intriguing linear leitmotif of almost awkward yet sinuous arabesques running through the painting. This motif is personified in the odd plumes projecting from his daughter's hat, which Matisse himself may have designed.

109

OSKAR SCHLEMMER

b. Stuttgart, Germany, 1888
d. Baden-Baden, Germany, 1943

Race

1930
Oil on canvas
161.6 x 96.5 cm. (63 5/8 x 38 in.)
Gift of Philip Johnson
Acquisition no. 1939.365

The Bauhaus was a center for the study and practice of art and design founded in 1919 in Weimar, Germany, later moving to Dessau and then to Berlin. Part of a general post-World War I aesthetic sensibility, the Bauhaus continued but modified the fascination with technology that had emerged in the art movements of the early twentieth century. With the devastation of the war, man's blind faith in the beneficence of technology was shaken. Though some movements, such as Dada, consequently satirized and attacked technology in their work, other groups, including the Precisionists, Purists, Constructivists, and the Bauhaus believed technology could aid mankind if it were properly harnessed and controlled. This sense of control is evidenced in an art emphasizing purity, order, and geometry, characteristics that also conveniently reflect the efficiency and precision associated with both the operation and design of machines.

Beginning in 1920, Oskar Schlemmer was associated with the Bauhaus as its head of sculpture and theater design. In 1930, he executed *Race*, an archetypal piece. The work includes the streamlined, stylized, muscular figures that appear in nearly all of his work, inhabiting his typical land of geometric precision. As is often the case in Schlemmer's art, the figures seem less active than the space itself, and though the piece is entitled *Race*, the motion of the men emphasizes precision rather than speed. Instead, it is Schlemmer's manipulation of deep, perspectival space that creates a feeling of velocity.

Schlemmer, who seldom did pure abstraction, concentrated on the human form, because he felt that too much of modern life was dehumanizing. Despite the startling azure, emerald, and magenta colors which Schlemmer applies with an expressive, feathery stroke, these efficient, muscular, ostensibly somnambulent figures seem to be a type lacking in individuality, personality, and consequently, humanity. But this sense of emptiness imbues them with qualities of mysticism and spiritualism, and they strike us as a breed akin to de Chirico's mannequins or to Léger's idealized, classicized, and mechanized men. As Schlemmer described them, they are "Dionysian in origin, Appollonian in manifestation, symbol of a unity of nature and spirit."

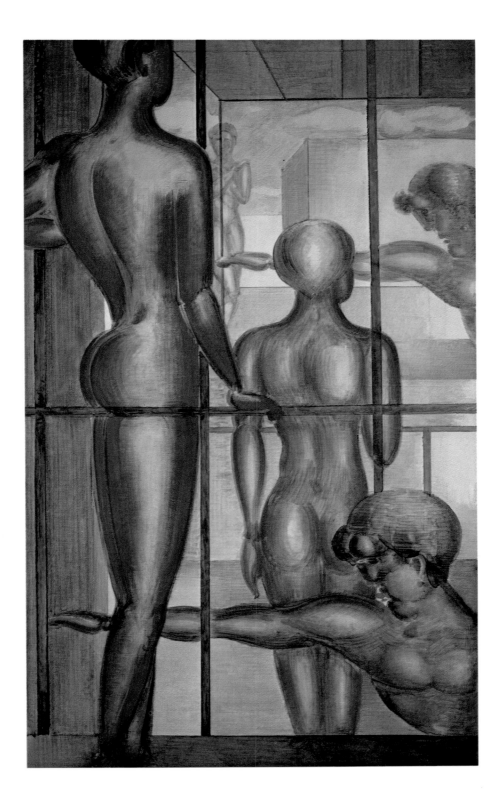

PIET MONDRIAN

b. Amersfoort, Holland, 1872
d. New York, 1944

Composition in Blue and White

1935
Oil on canvas
104.1 x 96.5 cm. (41 x 38 in.)
The Ella Gallup Sumner and
    Mary Catlin Sumner Collection
Acquisition no. 1936.338

Purity, spareness, and ultimate geometric abstraction are the characteristics most often associated with the work of Piet Mondrian. He arrived at this unique aesthetic position, however, after a period of painstaking investigation into a variety of phenomena, pictorial and otherwise. His early works, for example, are landscapes, done first in an Impressionist manner, and later in an Expressionist style reminiscent of the approach of his countryman Vincent van Gogh. But as he explored the world around him, he began to recognize that its basic visual units were horizontal and vertical: that is, horizon lines (ever so prominent in Holland), against which cross the perpendiculars of objects such as architecture and trees. During a stay in Paris between 1911 and 1914, Mondrian saw the art of Cubism, and it appeared to him that this most radical development in art was equally obsessed with horizontal/vertical juxtapositions. As if these two sources of inspiration weren't enough, Mondrian was influenced by the mystical, spiritual philosophy of Theosophy, which implied that there was an essential, underlying dynamism to reality analogous to the rigorous regularity of geometry. Thus, Mondrian was impelled by multiple sources toward an art that concomitantly referred to the structures of nature, art, and the cosmos.

By the late teens, Mondrian's style was also fundamental to the foundation of the De Stijl movement in Holland. De Stijl adopted Mondrian's absolute principles of the intersection of the vertical and horizontal, and the use of only primary colors, all arranged asymmetrically in order to create an art of "dynamic equilibrium." These requirements were to be applied to all the arts—painting, sculpture, architecture, and design. The great debt the world owes to Mondrian's principles is readily observable today in the buildings, furniture, graphics, and murals that now surround us. Therefore, paintings such as *Composition in Blue and White* should be seen as more than just a masterly formal arrangement. They represent basic inquiries into nature, art, and reality and function as models for the creation of many of the objects of our world.

112

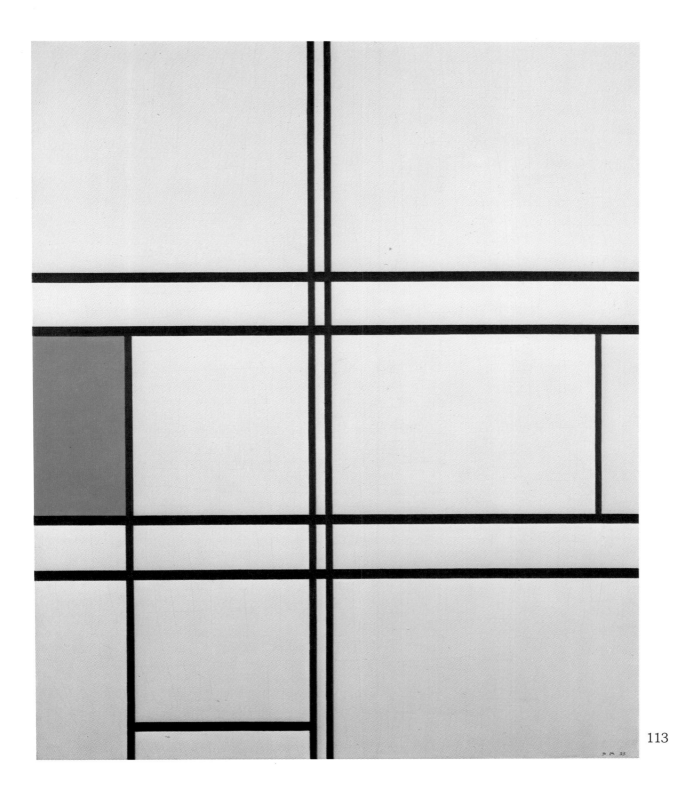

113

BALTHUS

b. Paris, 1908

The Bernese Hat

1938–39
Oil on canvas
91.8 x 72.8 cm. (36 1/8 x 28 11/16 in.)
The Ella Gallup Sumner and
  Mary Catlin Sumner Collection
Acquisition no. 1940.26

Born into an artistic family, Balthasar Klossowski de Rola, known as Balthus, forged a unique style based on precise rendering and the sometimes strange juxtaposition of objects to create an atmosphere of magic and mystery. Although it is related in spirit to the Metaphysical art of Giorgio de Chirico and the veristic wing of Surrealism, Balthus's "magic realism" retains a firmer identification with the everyday world. Seldom do bizarre distortions of objects appear in his art, and rather than combining completely unrelated elements within one pictorial space (as do the Surrealists), Balthus incorporates entities which could conceivably operate as he describes them.

Balthus's most compelling works are his sensual portrayals of adolescent girls in interior settings. Often nude, invariably in alluring and seductive poses, these nubile young girls are smoldering cores of budding sexuality. In these provocative paintings, the home becomes a hothouse, and innocent activities, such as reading, homework, and music practice, are voyeuristically transformed into autoerotic events.

The Bernese Hat, though less explicit than these depictions of pubescent girls, still has an enigmatic, perhaps melancholic atmosphere. Perhaps a portrait of Balthus's wife, the work is composed predominantly of somber, muted hues, with the exception of the mustard-yellow hat. Stylistically, it recalls some of the portraits of Gustave Courbet. The svelte figure is portrayed with a lost, disconnected expression, and her dreamy appearance is accentuated by the diagonal axis of her torso and head and the brooding light-and-dark bisection of her face.

115

PABLO PICASSO

b. Malaga, 1881
d. Mougins, 1973

The Painter

1934
Oil on canvas
98.3 x 80.2 cm. (38 $^{11}/_{16}$ x 31 $^{9}/_{16}$ in.)
The Ella Gallup Sumner and
   Mary Catlin Sumner Collection
Acquisition no. 1953.215

Pablo Picasso's career as an artist was extraordinary. He was an accomplished painter, sculptor, draftsman, printmaker, and set designer, and he is credited with pioneering (or helping to found) major modern developments including Cubism, collage, and construction. Although major formal innovations in modern art are attributed to Picasso, these compositional matters were often at the service of his subjects, and Picasso's art frequently explores the relationship between art and life and expresses his deeply felt concern for the human condition.

The Painter, one in a series of Picasso's works on the artist and his model, was inspired, in part, by his designs for the Balzac novel Le Chef d'oeuvre inconnu. It wittily addresses the issues of the interplay between nature and art. For instance, the model is a highly altered and dislocated figure suggestive of the forms of Picasso's art of the period; she appears to have been transformed by the artist even before he has approached the canvas. The primarily flat, strangely colored, sweeping, curvilinear forms are attenuations and distortions of the figure which are reordered to create an arrangement of complicated echoing and rhyming lines and shapes while retaining associations with their source. Yet, there is no denying the monstrousness of the model, and she is, to some extent, a reflection of Picasso's venomous attitude toward women (note the emphasis on and enlargement of sexual parts) during a time when his own amorous entanglements were complex and often frustrating. Moreover, these biomorphic shapes attest to Picasso's interest in the emerging Surrealist movement, for they seem to be the products of the automatistic techniques which the Surrealists believed were a revelation of the unconscious. Furthermore, what can perhaps be seen as a mutilation of the figure may also stem both from the Surrealist encouragement to give vent to one's desires, be they sadistic or otherwise, and their association between love and violence with the corollary that "beauty can only be convulsive."

In contrast to the elaborate and grotesque model is the bland, simplified painter. His somnolent demeanor may imply that interior vision and imagination are superior to the optical or purely perceptual; the artist looks at his model and sees her essence, not just her surface. The model is, ultimately, a far more mesmerizing figure than the painter. Picasso reminds us that the best art does not necessarily improve on nature, but may distort and recast it.

Other trenchant visual messages and puns include Picasso's belief in the morphology of forms; for instance, breasts and fruit become interchangeable, fingers echo flowers in a vase, while the vase itself echoes anatomical parts. Finally, it is worth noting that Picasso's "woman-monsters" re-surface later as sufferers of pain and anguish in his epic canvas chronicling the heinousness of war, Guernica.

117

SALVADOR DALI

b. Fugueras, Catalonia, 1904

Apparition of face and fruit-dish on a beach

1938
Oil on canvas
114.3 x 143.8 cm. (45 x 56 $5/8$ in.)
The Ella Gallup Sumner and
   Mary Catlin Sumner Collection
Acquisition no. 1939.269

Surrealism was an art movement founded in Paris in 1924 by the French poet André Breton. Breton gathered around him a group of artists, writers, and filmmakers to carry out the Surrealist credo of exalting the powers of the imagination. In their artistic endeavors, the Surrealists sought to break down the dichotomy between the real and the imaginary, between states of waking and dreaming, and between fact and fantasy. As a result, reality would be expanded while the powers of the imagination would be infinitely increased. Intrigued by the theories of Sigmund Freud, the Surrealists felt that the imagination could best be unleashed by tapping the workings of the unconscious, for the unconscious was the true heart of reality.

Of all the Surrealist artists, Salvador Dali is perhaps the best known. A highly flamboyant character, he explored the most bizarre themes in his art. He was a technical virtuoso, and the obsessive detail and clarity of his forms make even the most outlandish images appear believable. Executed according to a procedure he called the "paranoiac-critical method," Dali's paintings were described as "hand-painted dream photographs."

Apparition of face and fruit-dish on a beach illustrates his fascination with double images. As mentioned above, dualities intrigued the Surrealists and, in Freudian terms, objects or words or images often had double or multiple meanings. Here, Dali fuses a face with a dish or goblet, while the body of a dog is simultaneously a landscape and an arrangement of fruit. Doubles abound: for instance, the dog's snout masquerades as a sandy path or field, his eye is also a tunnel in a rock formation, and his collar becomes a viaduct through which water flows. Embedded in this dog-landscape crossbreed are a profusion of phantasmagorical images, or, to explain it as a Surrealist might, lurking beneath and attached to the surface of reality are other multiple layers of reality and fantasy. The painting is even signed Gala Salvador Dali, since Dali felt that his wife Gala was, in some respects, his missing half, his alter ego, and his double.

118

GIORGIO DE CHIRICO

b. Volus, Greece, 1888
d. Rome, 1978

The Endless Voyage

1914
Oil and chalk on canvas
88.9 x 40.3 cm. (35 x 15 7/8 in.)
The Philip L. Goodwin Collection
Acquisition no. 1958.221

Giorgio de Chirico intuits poetry and mystery in the objects of the everyday world. In his art, he extracts this poetry and mystery through odd perspectives, isolation and intensification of objects, and unusual juxtapositions.

The Endless Voyage is a typically strange de Chirico, containing elements common to his oeuvre, many of which may appear for the first time in this painting. They include: a classical sculpture fragment, a blackboard dotted with mathematical and geometrical formulas suggestive of perspective systems, images of towers, a mannequin (here cloaked in classical garb), and paintings within a painting. The precise inspiration for and meaning of each of these images are uncertain, but some speculation is possible. For example, the source of the towers was actual Medieval and Renaissance structures, and in customary fashion, de Chirico saw them as powerful, nearly animate forces in the Italian townscape. The notated blackboard may refer to the rigorous perspectival foundation of much Italian architecture and town planning, and de Chirico himself manipulates perspective in his works for eerie effects. The painting within a painting has potential autobiographic associations, but in causing the spectator to realize that an image within the work is actually a part of another piece, de Chirico creates confusion about the relationship between art and reality. Further complexity results from his clever application of chalk onto raw canvas to depict the central figure.

Finally, the sculptural fragment and the mannequin both show de Chirico's fascination with human surrogates. Part of a contemporary preoccupation with ersatz men in art and literature, de Chirico's naked mannequins or statues could be suggestive of the exposed man, stripped of his facade; or conversely, they could be thought of as an empty shell, all surface and no essence. In addition, here, de Chirico's mannequin is fitted with a lone eye, a symbol of the seer.

In any event, the true impact of de Chirico's work results less from the deciphering of individual symbols than from the anxious and enigmatic quality of the whole. In this spirit, the Surrealists were mesmerized by de Chirico's early art, for in its exultation of mystery, its belief in the hidden, higher states of objects, and its ability to evoke poetry through unlikely juxtapositions, it was a precursor to the Surrealist sensibility.

121

JOAN MIRÓ

b. Barcelona, 1893

Painting

1933
Oil on canvas
130.5 x 163.9 cm. (51 3/8 x 64 1/2 in.)
The Ella Gallup Sumner and
    Mary Catlin Sumner Collection
Acquisition no. 1934.40

While we tend to think of the major developments in modern art in the early twentieth century as being French, it is interesting to note that two of the key artists of Cubism—Pablo Picasso and Juan Gris—as well as two main figures of Surrealism—Salvador Dali and Joan Miró—were of Spanish origin. Miró, who settled in Paris in 1920, is the artist most representative of the abstract wing of Surrealism, which was divided into two pictorial camps. One wing—the veristic or realistic group—produced works that contained operable space inhabited by carefully delineated, representational, but often hallucinatory imagery, best illustrated by Salvador Dali's "hand-painted dream photograph" paintings. The other wing, greatly interested in the unconscious, executed works of a more abstract nature, in which a kind of free-play or doodling, called "automatism," was the initial motivating force.

Miró, an abstract Surrealist, often allowed an unconscious scrawl or an accidental drip or spill on the canvas to determine the development of the painting. Invariably, these random, haphazard inspirations were transformed as the work proceeded. What emerges is the kind of imagery we have in *Painting*. Color, often bright in Miró's work, is subdued in this piece. Space is relatively flat and amorphous; in it float wriggling, linear forms defining curious creatures. For example, in the lower right, we have a male-female hybrid, somewhat animal-like, with breasts hanging from its streamlined body and a phallic, protruding hairy extension, suggesting both male and female sexual organs. Other evocative and ambiguous forms populate the work. Nearly all are organic or biomorphic in shape, and all cavort in the canvas to create a libidinous, liberated "polymorphous perverse" world of fantasy.

MAX ERNST

b. Bruhl, 1891
d. Paris, 1976

Europe After the Rain

1940–42
Oil on canvas
54.8 x 147.8 cm. (21 $^{9}/_{16}$ x 58 $^{3}/_{16}$ in.)
The Ella Gallup Sumner and
   Mary Catlin Sumner Collection
Acquisition no. 1942.281

The events of World War II inspired numerous important works of art. Max Ernst, a German native living in France during the war, was interned in a concentration camp, and this event, along with the general horrors of the world conflict, inspired several of his important pieces. Among these is *Europe After the Rain*. The imagery of the painting is harrowing. As its title implies, the painting portrays a bizarre landscape which has been devastated, or more appropriately, transmogrified, by a rain of bombs, chemicals, and other insidious weapons. But this landscape appears ready to seek revenge on a now mutant mankind, who once used terrible technologies to conduct warfare and made nature his innocent victim. The landscape seems frighteningly animate, a kind of corrosive nature that envelops man and the artifacts of his civilization. Eerie forms are matched by disturbing colors, as a vaporous blue sky with greasy clouds serves as a backdrop for the sickly greens, charred reds, and burnt ochres of the landscape.

The chilling forcefulness of Ernst's apocalyptic vision was a product of the pictorial techniques being explored by the Surrealists. Ernst, who began his career as one of Germany's leading Dada artists and then settled in Paris in 1922, about the time Surrealism emerged, was intrigued by accidental approaches in art. Such methods include decalcomania, *grattage*, and *frottage*; in the first, pigment is allowed to drip down a manipulated canvas; in the second, paint is scraped onto the surface of a work with smooth or irregular tools; and in the third, texture is created by rubbing pigment across a canvas under which bumpy objects have been placed. Clearly, the textures, drips, odd shapes, and scrumbled surfaces of *Europe After the Rain* attest to Ernst's aleatory experiments. Though his lush vegetal works of this period were partly the result of the revival of interest in Henri Rousseau's oneiric landscapes, these images, done in response to war, seem to augur the atom bomb and its attendant horror.

The American Collection

YARMOUTH, PLYMOUTH COLONEY

Prince-Howes Court Cupboard

1665–70
Oak, maple, and pine
142.2 x 129.5 x 57.2 cm. (56 x 51 x 22 1/2 in.)
Gift of J. Pierpont Morgan
Acquisition no. 1926.289

This massive court cupboard is among the finest examples of American colonial furniture. Its ornamentation demonstrates the full range of seventeenth-century techniques: the surface is enriched by relief moldings, carving, and various lathe-turned elements. This variety indicates that the cupboard was produced by several artisans working in concert under the direction of one master. The joining and other details are distinctly American, but the overall style, with its highly regulated geometric patterns, is closely related to English and Dutch late Renaissance furniture. Indeed, it was once thought to have been imported to America from England, since early colonial craftsmen were then considered incapable of making such a sophisticated piece. More recently, Wallace Nutting and other scholars of American furniture have proved the fully American provenance of the cupboard.

Its original owner was Thomas Prence (or Prince). He arrived in America on the *Fortune*, the ship that followed the *Mayflower*, and in 1634 was elected Governor of the Plymouth colony. Prence retained this office through repeated elections, and became not only one of the wealthiest but also one of the most respected men of the colony. It is likely that the court cupboard was commissioned when the Governor built his new house around 1668. He died in 1673, and his will of that year stipulates, "I give unto my said loving wife my best bed and the furniture there unto appertaining, and the Court Cubberd that stands in the new Parlour." His widow, Mary Howes Prence, left it to her grandson Prence Howes, and it remained in the family until this century.

The cupboard is in a remarkably complete state of preservation; only a few details have been replaced. While it must have been made in the Governor's district in Yarmouth, it is the equal of any work made in Boston, then the most prosperous American city. Unfortunately no joiners' business records from this period survive, and it is impossible to know the exact process by which such an elaborate piece would have been designed and constructed. Nonetheless, the Prince-Howes court cupboard stands as evidence to the sophistication that could be found in even the earliest American furniture.

A.L.G.

DEVONSHIRE

Joined Oak Chest

Ca. 1650–80
Oak
82.5 x 138.4 x 68 cm. (32 1/2 x 54 1/2 x
   26 3/4 in.)
J. J. Goodwin Fund
Acquisition no. 1981.3

128

This newly acquired chest is a particularly welcome addition to the Wadsworth Atheneum collection as it is representative of a provincial style of English workmanship that had an immediate following in colonial America. The tripartite panels and foliate relief are typical of Devonshire cabinetmaking of the late Commonwealth and Restoration periods. This chest can be compared to the Hadley chest on the facing page, and it is easy to see how this kind of shallow, balanced relief-work has been translated into an inventive style. The chest is made entirely of oak, and is unmarred by repairs or replacements. The general austerity of the overall design indicates that this piece was intended for a middle-class household rather than one of the renowned stately homes of England.

A.L.G.

MASSACHUSETTS

Hadley Box

Ca. 1680–1700
Oak and pine
22.3 x 65.4 x 43.9 cm. (8 3/4 x
    25 3/4 x 17 1/4 in.)
Gift of J. Pierpont Morgan
Acquisition no. 1926.352

Hadley Chest

1690–1700
Pine
90.1 x 112.5 x 51 cm. (35 1/2 x 44 1/4 x
    20 in.)
Gift of J. Pierpont Morgan
Acquisition no. 1926.303

The Hadley boxes and chests of colonial New England are derived from regional English joinery traditions. They are identified by their low-relief, foliate carving, made up of tulip and vine motifs. The initials of the owners, and occasionally the date of manufacture, are frequently inscribed in the center of the decoration, as in the examples in the Wadsworth Atheneum. The initials on the box may belong to the Reverend Benjamin Colton of Longmeadow, Massachusetts. The initials on the chest have yet to be identified. Hadley boxes and chests were frequently paired as they are here; but these two examples were made by different craftsmen. Thus there must have been a widespread diffusion of Hadley-type decoration in the Connecticut Valley. The name Hadley has been given to these chests since 1882, when a local collector discovered one in Hadley, Massachusetts.

129

A.L.G.

ATTRIBUTED TO CHARLES GILLAM

Place and date of birth unknown
d. Saybrook, Connecticut, 1727

Chest of Drawers

Ca. 1700–27
Oak and tulipwood
111.8 x 108.9 x 51.4 cm. (44 x
    42 7/8 x 20 1/4 in.)
Gift of J. Pierpont Morgan
Acquisition no. 1926.327

While the Hadley chests are among the best known examples of early American furniture, the painted chests from the Saybrook and Guilford areas of coastal Connecticut are also fine pieces of Colonial joinery. The present example is painted with a standard floral motif made up of tulips, vines, thistles, and roses, and is further embellished by crowns, partridges, and a *fleur de lis*. These patterns are probably derived from English print sources, but where they once had specific reference, they are applied freely here. The same decoration can be found on Saybrook chests in the Ford Museum in Dearborn, Michigan, and the Metropolitan Museum of Art in New York.

The attribution of these chests to Charles Gillam was made in 1958 by William L. Warren. In an article published in the Connecticut Historical Society Bulletin, Warren traces the provenance of these works back to the Guilford-Saybrook area, and demonstrates that Gillam, a joiner, would have had the materials for the design and decoration of such chests. In the inventory of his estate were the items "a painted chest with drawers, a parcel of collours, boxes, brushes and gums etc." However, so little is known about Gillam that this attribution must remain hypothetical.

A.L.G.

131

SAMUEL LOOMIS

b. Colchester, Connecticut, 1748
d. Pettipaug, Connecticut, 1814

Chest-on-Chest

Ca. 1771
Mahogany
223 x 114 x 66 cm. (87 3/4 x
    44 7/8 x 26 in.)
Gift of Mr. and Mrs. Arthur L.
    Shipman, Jr.
Acquisition no. 1967.40

The provenance of this exceptionally fine chest-on-chest can be traced back to its first owner, Jonathan Deming. Deming was a merchant in Colchester, where he built a family mansion in 1771, and it is likely that this piece was commissioned for the new home. In a 1788 inventory of the Deming estate, the chest was identified as "Samuel Loomis work," and was valued at the then exceptionally high price of £16. There is no documentation of Loomis's training, but contemporary chest-on-chests and high chests of the same style can be found in southeastern Connecticut and the Connecticut Valley. The design is made up of two separate units, one chest being fitted on top of the other. The ornamentation is modelled expertly, and includes carved shells, fans, rope columns, incised carving, and a scrolled base—all of which is triumphantly capped by an elaborate broken scroll pediment. As this is one of the only pieces securely documented to Loomis's shop, it is a key work upon which all other attributions depend.

A.L.G.

ELIPHELET CHAPIN

b. Somers, Connecticut, 1741
d. Hartford, 1807

High Chest

Ca. 1771
Cherry and pine
206 x 100 x 50 cm. (81 1/16 x 39 3/8 x
    19 11/16 in.)
Gift of Mr. and Mrs. Robert P. Butler
Acquisition no. 1964.146

This high chest, with its suave and elegant decoration, is a typical American translation of European Rococo. Eliphelet Chapin has instilled a sense of élan and movement into this high chest by attenuating the proportions and by shaping the legs and pediment into tensile curves that seem possessed of their own organic energy. The unique acroterium (the asymmetrical cartouche that crowns the piece) gives the chest a Rococo flair not usually found in Connecticut furniture like the Loomis chest on this page. Chapin assimilated the style made popular by Thomas Chippendale in England, during a sojourn in Philadelphia, then the most sophisticated city in America. However, Chapin's work also retains a Connecticut character in that his pieces rarely show the cosmopolitan variety and wealth of carving found in Philadelphia furniture.

A.L.G.

132

AARON CHAPIN

b. Somers, Connecticut, 1751
d. Hartford(?), 1838

Sideboard

1804
Inlaid mahogany and pine
104.8 x 199.4 x 66.6 cm. (41 $^1/_2$ x
78 $^1/_2$ x 26 $^1/_4$ in.)
Gift of Frederick A. Robbins
Acquisition no. 1952.189

Aaron Chapin was second cousin to Eliphelet Chapin, the progenitor of a large family of Connecticut furniture makers in the Hartford area. Aaron served as an apprentice and journeyman to Eliphelet, and in 1783 set himself up as an independent cabinetmaker in Hartford. By 1800 the shop had grown in size and prominence, and the following advertisement appeared in the 1803 *Connecticut Courant*, "AARON CHAPIN . . . has on hand elegant Sideboards, made in the newest fashion, and of the best mahogany. . . . He flatters himself that by having the best of timber, and workmen, he shall be able to furnish setts of furniture on short notice, that shall be both handsome and good."

The sideboard in the Wadsworth Atheneum demonstrates Aaron's considerable skill. The "newest fashion" mentioned in the advertisement refers to the Neoclassical style just then coming into popularity. While Eliphelet chose the Rococo Chippendale pieces of Philadelphia as his models, Aaron's work is done in the patriotic Roman style of the Early National period. This style was popularized by the English designer George Heppelwhite, whose work was published in an illustrated trade catalogue with descriptions and specifications. The reduced geometry and the interplay between convex and concave surfaces on the front of the sideboard are typical of Heppelwhite design, and a similar serpentine style can be found in Hartford furniture by Aaron's contemporaries. An unusual though not unique feature of this piece is the eight legs; six was generally the preferred number. The classically inspired inlay is yet another feature of the new and more austere taste.

This sideboard is of particular importance because it is securely documented, unlike most of Aaron's work. It had remained in the family that first commissioned the piece, and when it was donated to the Wadsworth Atheneum, the original 1804 bill of sale was also included. It was made out to Frederic Robbins of Rocky Hill, Hartford County, and the sideboard's cost was the then formidable price of $68.00.

A.L.G.

BENJAMIN WEST

b. Springfield, Pennsylvania, 1738
d. London, 1820

Saul and the Witch of Endor

1777
Oil on canvas
50.8 x 65.4 cm. (19 15/16 x 25 3/4 in.)
Bequest of Mrs. Clara Hinton Gould
Acquisition no. 1948.186

Benjamin West was in the vanguard of two major developments of late eighteenth- and early nineteenth-century art: Neoclassicism and Romanticism. Born in the Colonies, of modest means, West received support from some admiring Philadelphians to study abroad. His first stop in Europe was Italy, where he encountered the contemporary revival of classicism. In direct contact with antique artifacts (Pompeii and Herculaneum had recently been excavated) and having met the German archeologist and antiquarian Johann Joachim Wincklemann, West became a leading proponent of classicism in art. This antique renaissance was part of the Enlightenment spirit, which valued the order and rationality of the classical world and the morality of ancient philosophy. Upon moving to England in 1763, where he permanently settled, West produced several major canvases based on classical history or mythology, done in a frieze-like, orderly style, with sculptural, idealized figures rhetorically arranged so as to best convey moral messages.

West's success as an artist eventually led to his appointment as official History Painter to King George III. The notoriety of West's career as an American boy who made good in the Old World resulted in his becoming the magnet for aspiring American artists who wished to study abroad. It was West who aided Copley in England; others, including John Trumbell, Samuel F. B. Morse, Ralph Earl, and Washington Allston all came to work at West's studio, which also housed a fine art collection.

However, West eventually subordinated the clarity and order of his Neoclassicism to give his work an excitement and mystery that anticipated a new artistic development—Romanticism. West's interest in Romanticism was most likely inspired by Edmund Burke's writings on the sublime. To imbue art with awe and wonder, Burke stated, the artist should select miraculous subjects and depict them in an obscure, nuanced, and ambiguous fashion. West's *Saul and the Witch of Endor* is painted in this spirit. Biblical and Shakespearian scenes had become more important in West's work, and here he picks a particularly frightening Old Testament event: the Witch of Endor summons the ghost of the dead prophet Samuel so that King Saul may question him about a battle in which Saul will meet his own death. The painting, primarily dark at the edges and vaporous and apparitional at the core, with its scene of terror and mystery in the face of the supernatural, fulfills the requirements of the Burkean sublime.

JOHN SINGLETON COPLEY

b. Boston, 1738
d. London, 1815

Mrs. Seymour Fort (?)

Ca. 1778
Oil on canvas
125.7 x 100.7 cm. (49 1/2 x 39 5/8 in.)
Acquisition no. 1901.34

Some mystery surrounds John Singleton Copley's portrait of *Mrs. Seymour Fort*. First, identification of the sitter as Mrs. Fort has still not been positively established, and even if it is she, we know little about her or her husband. There is also conjecture about when and where the portrait was executed, but it seems clear that it dates from Copley's London period, around 1778.

Since portraiture was the most popular form of painting in America during the Colonial period, and Copley was regarded as America's best portraitist, he naturally became one of the country's most famous artists. Copley's renown rested on his ability to achieve remarkable effects in his portraits: for a pragmatic society, he could provide images of striking realism; for the aristocracy, who could best afford portraits, he painted his subjects with trappings that signified their status.

Although he began painting in the early 1750s, his most famous portraits date from the 1760s up through his departure for Europe in 1774. The most striking characteristics of these pieces are their clarity of form and their textural verisimilitude. Copley imparts a stunning, reflective luster to the surfaces of objects. Furthermore, while many of his figures' faces, accoutrements, and surroundings seem to be stamped from similar molds, he imbues his figures with individual personality and purpose.

Mrs. Seymour Fort, done after Copley left the Colonies, marks a new approach in his art. Crispness of form is subordinated to overall effects; brushstrokes, once concealed, now grow looser and more revealing. A more sophisticated understanding of light and shadow provides unity through contrasting, yet eliding pictorial relationships, distinct from the insistent equalization of forces in his earlier work. Copley has adopted the "grand painterliness" of European portraiture, but his interest in texture remains and his sitters still engage in identifying tasks and possess the personality of his earlier work. On the other hand, it is amusing to note that Mrs. Seymour Fort's dress is nearly identical to that worn by another Copley sitter—Mrs. Isaac Royall.

138

RALPH EARL

b. Worcester County, Massachusetts,
    1751
d. Bolten, Connecticut, 1801

Chief Justice Oliver Ellsworth and His Wife, Abigail Wolcott

1792
Oil on canvas
192.9 x 220.3 cm. (75 $^{15}/_{16}$ x 86 $^{3}/_{4}$
    in.)
Gift of Ellsworth Heirs
Acquisition no. 1903.7

The career of art, as practiced in America in its early years, could be rewarding if the artist were an adequate portraitist. Ralph Earl is typical of any number of early American portrait painters, who probably had little formal training and simply learned their trade as they worked. After a brief foray into history painting, Earl, who was a Tory sympathizer, was forced to flee the Colonies and travelled to England in 1778. Not unlike the work of John Singleton Copley, which became more painterly and less crisp and clear after exposure to European art, Earl's work underwent a similar transformation. His stiff, awkward, but forthright portrayals are replaced by more sophisticated and colorful works with figures more properly modelled and features more carefully rendered.

Chief Justice Oliver Ellsworth and His Wife, Abigail Wolcott is an example of this later period. Earl returned to the United States about 1785, where with the lessons of Benjamin West, Reynolds, and Gainsborough in hand, he received portrait commissions from some of America's most distinguished citizens. Ironically, his main sitters were American patriots, and Chief Justice Ellsworth, delegate to the Continental Congress and head of the Supreme Court, was also a framer and signer of the Constitution. As is typical of portraits of this era, where trappings transmit information, Ellsworth holds a copy of the Constitution. He and his wife are seated in the Washington Room of their home, so named because of a visit by America's first president. Since the house was such a pleasant structure, Earl had no compunction about representing it twice, and the view out the window contains an image of the Ellsworth homestead. The house, which was a working farm, still stands today in East Windsor, Connecticut, the birthplace of Ellsworth's wife.

140

JOHN VANDERLYN

b. Kingston, New York, 1775
d. Kingston, New York, 1852

Death of Jane McCrea

Ca. 1804
Oil on canvas
67.3 x 81.3 cm. (32 x 26 1/2 in.)
Purchased from a subscription
Acquisition no. 1855.4

Early in his career, John Vanderlyn painted a portrait of Aaron Burr which so impressed Burr that he became the artist's patron. In the late eighteenth and early nineteenth centuries, it was customary for well-educated American painters to travel to England to study with the great artists and at the fine schools of the Old World. Since Burr, however, had little love for England and was something of a Francophile, he sponsored Vanderlyn on a journey to Paris, and the artist became the first major American to train on the continent rather than on British soil.

What Vanderlyn observed and learned in France was crucial to the painting of *Death of Jane McCrea*. He encountered Neoclassical art, a style pioneered and popularized by Jacques Louis David which, in reaction to the frivolousness of the Rococo and in sympathy with the philosophy of the Enlightenment, revived classical models to create an art of order and clarity. Though the Indians in this painting, about to scalp Jane McCrea, are hardly meant to personify Rousseau's notion of the "noble savage," they have well-defined musculature and are posed in a manner that harks back to the antique. The victim, Jane McCrea, wears a garment whose crisp folds suggest classical statuary and whose face, drawn in the linear style that perfuses the entire piece, is shown in sharp profile, typical of classicism.

Some confusion still surrounds the story of Jane McCrea. We do know that she was preparing to rendezvous with her soldier fiancé when Indians, paid by the British either to escort the woman or to collect scalps, sheared and killed McCrea. If they were her escorts, her murder came about because the two Indians, inflamed by Jane's beauty, were battling over who should be her prime protector. In any case, the subject became popular with poets and painters, and was commonly exploited to fuel anti-British feelings. This particular painting was commissioned to accompany Joel Barlow's description of the event in his American saga, *Columbiad*. In composition, *Death of Jane McCrea* is reminiscent of scenes of the flagellation of Christ. It also takes on the feeling of a cliff-hanger, with her fiancé running futilely to her rescue.

Done in Paris in 1804, *Death of Jane McCrea* was the first painting of autochthonous American history shown at the Paris Salon. The painting, one of about fifty works purchased from the defunct American Academy of Fine Arts in New York, was part of the first major acquisition by the Wadsworth Atheneum after its founding.

143

ASA AMES

Active in Buffalo and Evans, New
   York, 1823–51

Seated Female Figure with Lamb and Cup

1850
Polychromed yellow poplar
74.2 cm. high (24 1/4 in.)
Bequest of Roscoe Nelson Gray in
   Memory of Roscoe Nelson Daton
   Gray and Rene Gabrielle Gray
Acquisition no. 1978.3

Few folk artists were trained or worked in the fashion of established or "professional" artists. Instead, they were generally craftsmen
who also chose to carve, paint, whittle, and cast a variety of art objects
that served both utilitarian and decorative purposes. While styles vary
greatly throughout the many American examples of folk art, several
characteristics unite the genre: a certain naivity of execution, a preference for bold colors and schematic compositions, and, frequently, a
kind of emotional intensity not found in the approved, academic art of
that time. Little is known about these artists, and the undocumented life
of Asa Ames is no exception. We do know that he carved this curious
piece as a memorial. The date 1850 has been inscribed on the stool's
base, and it is likely that it was dedicated to the memory of Sarah
Reliance and Ann Augusta, the infant daughters of Colonel James H.
Ayer, who died in an epidemic. The lamb, a symbol of innocence, was a
frequent motif on children's gravestones of this period. The ribbon,
drapery, and proffered cup are similarly related to funerary imagery of
the early decades of the nineteenth century. However, while these
monuments typically show the children either asleep or at prayer, the
child illustrated here regards the viewer with fixed alertness, challenging
the oblivion of death.

144

A.L.G.

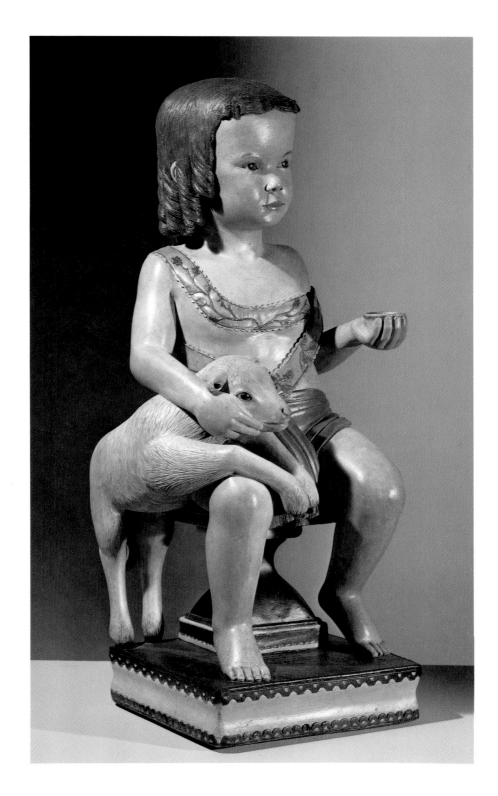

145

REMBRANDT PEALE

b. Bucks County, Pennsylvania, 1778
d. Philadelphia, 1860

Self-Portrait

1834
Oil on panel
61 x 51 cm. (24 x 20 1/8 in.)
William B. and Mary Arabella
   Goodwin Collection
Acquisition no. 1950.778

Son of the famous artist, scientist, naturalist, inventor, and entrepreneur Charles Wilson Peale, Rembrandt Peale, along with his brothers Raphaelle, Rubens, and Titian, was intended to live up to his name and enter the field of art. All the members of the Peale family (several of the sisters were talented still-life painters) saw art as a money-making proposition, and the family history is replete with all sorts of financial schemes. For example, in 1786 C. W. Peale established the Peale Museum in Philadelphia, one of the country's first, which exhibited not only art but also fossils, skeletons, stuffed animals, flora, and fauna. He also founded the Columbianum Academy, progenitor of the Pennsylvania Academy of Fine Arts, America's oldest art school.

In this spirit, Rembrandt launched the Peale Museum and Gallery of Fine Arts in Baltimore, which contained a hall of portraits of distinguished men. Hoping to make the gallery a success, he had no qualms about mixing art and science. An inventor like his father, he demonstrated the benefits of gas lighting in the museum and later founded the Gas Light Company of Baltimore. In both of these ventures, Rembrandt proved to be a poor businessman and he suffered substantial financial losses.

The Peale family specialized in portraits, still lifes, and, in the case of Rembrandt, occasionally history painting. Though described as a "portrait factory," they made notable contributions to the field of portraiture and their still lifes are regarded as pioneering *trompe l'oeil* creations. Rembrandt Peale's *Self-Portrait* is a convincing and striking portrayal. The dark tones of the background and of the artist's fur-collared coat serve as a brilliant foil to the carefully modelled, meticulously detailed, animately glowing face. Peale also did a famous rendering of George Washington, in which the country's President appears to be peering out from an oval enclosure. Dubbed the "porthole" effect, this mode became increasingly popular among American portraitists. Since prestige accompanied portrayals of the "Founding Father," Gilbert Stuart, who painted some of the most famous pictures of the President, reacted to the increasing monopoly the Peale family had on depictions of Washington by writing to the First Lady that George was in danger of being "Pealed all around."

147

THOMAS COLE

b. Botton-Le-Moor, England, 1801
d. Catskill, New York, 1848

Scene from "The Last of the Mohicans," Cora Kneeling at the Feet of Tamenund

1827
Oil on canvas
64.4 x 89 cm. (25 3/8 x 35 1/16 in.)
Bequest of Alfred Smith
Acquisition no. 1868.3

The works of Thomas Cole are of special significance to the Wadsworth Atheneum. Daniel Wadsworth, founder of the museum, was one of Cole's major patrons. Cole's landscapes, which formed the nucleus of Wadsworth's holdings when the Atheneum was established, became the core around which one of the best collections of American nineteenth-century landscapes was built.

Often regarded as the "Father of American Landscape," Cole transformed this previously "minor mode" into the preeminent subject of artistic expression in America in the nineteenth century. In a country short on tradition and often indifferent to the arts, Cole discovered that the American wilderness could be a symbol capable of defining the American spirit, thus elevating to importance those artists and writers who best captured that spirit. He found drama and power in rugged frontier locales, and though he painted a variety of places, his association with the landscape along the Hudson River led to the label "The Hudson River School," which eventually came to designate several generations of American landscape artists.

The *Scene from "The Last of the Mohicans," Cora Kneeling at the Feet of Tamenund*, reveals that Cole, along with James Fenimore Cooper, whose novel inspired the painting, had an interest in indigenous American history. Though Cole selected a scene of great drama from the Cooper novel, he has emphasized the sensational landscape rather than the stirring narrative. Craggy, overhanging rocks lead back to soaring pinnacles. Towering peaks alternate with yawning chasms, as they recede into deep space. All is accentuated by powerful contrasts of light and shade. As aggrandized as the landscape is, Cole meticulously paints the most minor details, so that even individual leaves on trees are clearly visible. Amidst this grand panorama, Cooper's story is nestled. Truly, the events of history appear fleeting and insignificant in the face of the sublime majesty of nature. This was one of Daniel Wadsworth's favorite paintings, and he aptly described his awe before it: "I can hardly express my admiration—the Grand and magnificent Scenery—it speaks for itself."

THOMAS CHAMBERS

b. England, ca. 1808
d. Place unknown, after 1866

Niagara Falls

Ca. 1832–40
Oil on canvas
55.9 x 76.4 cm. (22 x 30 1/16 in.)
The Ella Gallup Sumner and
    Mary Catlin Sumner Collection
Acquisition no. 1943.99

One of the world's great wonders, Niagara Falls held as much attraction to nineteenth-century artists as it does to contemporary honeymooners. Many tried their hand at this most magnificent of scenes, including Thomas Cole, Frederick Edwin Church, John Trumbull, John Vanderlyn, John Frederick Kensett, and Albert Bierstadt. Cole, in his "Essay on American Scenery," eloquently described the magnetism of the Falls: "AND NIAGARA! that wonder of the world!— where the sublime and beautiful are bound together in an indissoluble chain. In gazing on it we feel as though a great void had been filled in our minds—our conceptions expand—we become a part of what we behold! At our feet the floods of a thousand rivers are poured out—the contents of vast inland seas. In its volume we conceive immensity; in its course, everlasting duration; in its impetuosity, uncontrollable power. These are the elements of its sublimity. Its beauty is garlanded around in the varied hues of the water, in the spray that ascends the sky, and in that unrivalled bow which forms a complete cincture round the unresting floods."

Thomas Chambers, who was labelled an American primitive, also portrayed the falls. Facts about his life and art remain scant, although some sixty-five works have been attributed to him. A painter of the land and the sea of America's Northwest, Chambers often worked from illustrations in books rather than directly from the site. As a result, the fairly common pictorial interpretation of being enveloped and awed by Niagara Falls is absent here, although a lone figure in the canvas stands captivated before this wonder of nature. Instead, the scene has been translated into a patterned arrangement of beguilingly colored, often sharply silhouetted flat forms. Chambers is no mean craftsman, however, as he cleverly contrasts bold darks and lights. Thus, spumes of bright water vie with dark rocks and trees to create a charming compositional tempo.

151

FREDERICK EDWIN CHURCH

b. Hartford, Connecticut, 1826
d. New York, 1900

Vale of St. Thomas, Jamaica

1867
Oil on canvas
122.7 x 215 cm. (48 5/16 x 84 5/8 in.)
The Elizabeth Hart Jarvis
   Colt Collection
Acquisition no. 1905.21

Of all the major nineteenth-century American landscape painters, Frederick Edwin Church was the most mesmerized by the overwhelming and the exotic. A native of Hartford and the son of Daniel Wadsworth's neighbor, Church took up study with Thomas Cole in the Catskills upon the recommendation of Wadsworth. A true disciple of Cole, he was to become one of the key figures of the second generation of the Hudson River School.

Like Cole, Church believed that nature revealed truth. For Church, this truth concerned science, religion, and philosophy, and the more spectacular the scene, the more profound were the truths unveiled. While Church found drama nearby in the Catskills and at Niagara Falls, he travelled from the Andes to the Arctic in search of the stupendous. Moreover, his journeys, like those of the scientist Charles Darwin, were greatly inspired by the writings of the German naturalist Alexander von Humboldt, who urged the exploration of the "inexhaustible treasures" of South America. As an "artist-naturalist," Church investigated and depicted nature, in part to fulfill Humboldt's demand to develop "knowledge of the works of creation, and an appreciation of their exalted grandeur."

Vale of St. Thomas, Jamaica, done for Hartford patron Elizabeth Hart Jarvis Colt, was the product of many sketches Church executed while on a voyage to Jamaica in 1865. With its viewpoint from above, this portrayal is actually an amalgam of many diverse sites joined to form a lush, tropical expanse. Despite its grandiose quality, Church still gives the most minute description of exotic flora and fauna. A brooding thunderstorm uniting land and sky provides the appropriate dramatic note, and the mysterious light, reminiscent of that in J. M. W. Turner's sublime art, further charges this sweeping, cinematic scene.

153

ALBERT BIERSTADT

b. Solingen, Nord Rhine-Westphalia, 1830
d. New York, 1902

In the Mountains

1867
Oil on canvas
91.9 x 127.7 cm (36 3/16 x 50 1/4 in.)
Gift of John J. Morgan in memory of his mother Juliet Pierpont Morgan
Acquisition no. 1923.253

The idea of "Manifest Destiny" embodied the American belief that westward expansion was divinely ordained. Expeditions to the American wilderness not only included explorers and trailblazers but artists, photographers, and writers as well. Perhaps America's most famous painter of the Western landscape was Albert Bierstadt. His grandiose, sometimes overblown, operatic depictions of this virgin terrain struck an understanding chord with an optimistic and aggressive America, and his ability to demonstrate pictorially that America had sites to rival those of Europe made him the nation's most successful artist of the 1860s.

In the Mountains of 1867 was completed from oil sketches made while Bierstadt was on a Western expedition. The work is characteristic of many of his wilderness scenes: from a placid lake rise sheer cliffs and towering peaks; the mountains intermingle with the sky, as if soaring toward the heavens. Links between sky and earth are reinforced through storm clouds which hover above the waterfalls that they fuel. The falls cascade from great heights to the lake below, which in turn reflects all the pictorial elements above it. Darker shades enframe a central core of active, misty light. All is at the service of the magnificent and the sublime.

JOHN FREDERICK KENSETT

b. Cheshire, Connecticut, 1816
d. New York, 1872

**Coast Scene with Figures
(Beverly Shore)**

1869
Oil on canvas
92.2 x 153 cm. (36 1/4 x 60 1/4 in.)
The Ella Gallup Sumner and
    Mary Catlin Sumner Collection
Acquisition no. 1942.345

The later generations of artists of the Hudson River School introduced changes in the approach to landscape that Thomas Cole, its first main practitioner, had established. One of these developments is well represented in the art of John Frederick Kensett, whose early work of dark, dense, intimate scenes suggests a more domesticated world than the wilds portrayed in Cole's painting. By the mid-1850s, a new style begins to emerge in Kensett's oeuvre that reaches maturity in works like *Coast Scene with Figures (Beverly Shore)*.

This style has been described as Luminism. It should be pointed out that the term "Luminism" is a much later invention of art scholars, used to categorize the pictorial characteristics of certain American artists primarily of the second half of the nineteenth century; never was the label mentioned by the artists themselves or by their contemporary critics. Nevertheless, the term has stuck, and Kensett's *Coast Scene with Figures (Beverly Shore)* is often regarded as an archetypal Luminist scene.

The painting is thought of as Luminist for a number of reasons. It is a tranquil, timeless, airless work, by virtue of its clear light, stable horizontal format, distillation of form, and arrested action. In this way, the artist stands before nature like the "transparent eyeball" of Emerson: a lens through which images are reflected with lucidity and purity. Through subordination of his will before nature, the artist more fully identifies or empathizes with the objects of the world, and thus he reveals them in his art with transcendent crystallinity and light. The quasi-mystical or religious foundations of such an approach are evident. Thus, Kensett's work, with its horizontal emphasis, has an almost crepuscular and reverent atmosphere. Tiny figures stand before the vastness of the ocean, in which waves seem frozen at the moment before breaking. Atmospheric perspective blurs the horizon line, and the painting appears divided into four nearly distinct compartments—sky, sea, sand, and rock—each referring to an elemental force of nature yet combining to assert an independent pictorial power.

157

WINSLOW HOMER

b. Boston, 1836
d. Prouts Neck, Maine, 1910

The Nooning

Ca. 1872
Oil on canvas
33.9 x 50.2 cm. (13 5/16 x 19 3/4 in.)
The Ella Gallup Sumner and
　Mary Catlin Sumner Collection
Acquisition no. 1947.1

Winslow Homer began his artistic career as an illustrator for *Harper's Weekly* in 1857. Later assigned as a correspondent at the front during the Civil War, Homer sketched numerous war scenes, many of which would serve as the basis for his first major oils. Pictorial documentation of the Civil War included not only drawings like these, but also important photographs. It is intriguing to compare Homer's treatment of the war with those of photographers, for Homer normally selected anecdotal, bloodless scenes as opposed to the grim and chilling chronicles found in the shots by Matthew Brady and Timothy O'Sullivan.

After the war, Homer turned his attention toward calmer scenes whose protagonists are often children, suggesting, perhaps, his hopes for an era of peace and innocence. Pictorially, Homer was particularly fascinated by characteristics of light. This interest may well have been reinforced after a trip to Europe in the late 1860s during which he probably encountered the pioneering experiments in light being conducted by the fledgling Impressionists.

The Nooning is a perfect example of a tranquil postwar scene in which investigation into the qualities of color and light play a large role. In *The Nooning*, the foreground of dark and drab greens is in shade, while a figure lies prone in a central patch of light. Fairly broad alternations of light and dark, punctuated by more active dapplings of sunshine, structure the work, which along with the noticeable brushstroke, tend to flatten the piece. But unlike the French Impressionists, Homer never completely dissolves the solidity of objects into pure dazzle and atmosphere. Moreover, Homer's training as an illustrator continued to operate throughout his career: he never lost his eye for the anecdotal or the dramatic. While *The Nooning*, like the contemporary stories of Mark Twain and Louisa May Alcott, deals with a childhood scene of play or leisure, Homer's later works, particularly those of the Maine coast, focus on man's difficult struggle with a harsh world and on the elemental forces of nature.

158

SANFORD ROBINSON GIFFORD

b. Greenfield, New York, 1823
d. New York, 1880

A Passing Storm in the Adirondacks

1866
Oil on canvas
95 x 138 cm. (37 3/8 x 54 3/8 in.)
The Elizabeth Hart Jarvis
   Colt Collection
Acquisition no. 1905.23

Like all the artists of the Hudson River School, Sanford Gifford's first love was nature. As a painter of landscape, he travelled extensively, seeking motifs suitable for depiction. He first went on walking tours of the Catskills, Adirondacks, and Berkshires, and expanded his horizons considerably with trips to the American West, Europe, and the Middle East. Because of its concentration on light and atmosphere, frequently horizontal orientation, purification of form, and overall serene mood, Gifford's art, along with that of John Frederick Kensett, Martin Heade, and Fritz Hugh Lane, has been called "Luminist." Luminism is the term employed by art historians in recent years to describe certain developments in late nineteenth-century American landscape, in which the artist so humbled himself before nature that his art demonstrates, through its clarity and light, a spiritual link with the objects of the world.

Gifford's *A Passing Storm in the Adirondacks* is not one of his classic Luminist pieces. Selection of a moving meteorological moment (although it is the calm before the storm) and a monumental site aligns him more with the dramatic pursuits of Thomas Cole, Frederick Edwin Church, and his friend Albert Bierstadt. In fact, there is much here that reminds us of Bierstadt's work. From a placid lake in which animals wade and drink rise magnificent peaks, bathed in veiled light, although the recession into space is less abrupt than that found in Bierstadt's paintings. Gifford's concern with atmospheric effects, which eventually became one of the key elements in his art, is also pronounced, and this concern with sky, clouds, and weather derives most likely from his exposure to the work of the British artists J. M. W. Turner and John Constable rather than to his American colleagues.

160

161

GEORGE INNESS

b. Newburgh, New York, 1825
d. Bridge-of-Allan, Scotland, 1894

Etretat

1875
Oil on canvas
75.8 x 114.2 cm. (29 7/8 x 44 15/16 in.)
The Ella Gallup Sumner and
   Mary Catlin Sumner Collection
Acquisition no. 1956.480

The town of Etretat was a popular haunt of French artists in the nineteenth century: Eugène Delacroix, Camille Corot, Gustave Courbet, and Claude Monet, to mention the most famous, all painted there. The American artist George Inness did approximately twenty paintings of this seaside resort, and this *Etretat* was completed in the United States, based on sketches and memories recorded during his third European sojourn.

Inness, though associated with the Hudson River School, adopted an attitude toward landscape quite different from that of Thomas Cole and Frederick Edwin Church. Peace, rather than drama, pervades his scenes, and while, as a devotee of Swedenborgianism, he believed in the spiritual value of landscape, his paintings stressed the virtues of contemplation and avoided the often bombastic didacticism of the major nineteenth-century American landscape artists.

The style of Inness's art changed throughout his career. Perhaps his most moving works date from the eighteen-eighties and nineties, when he suppressed details, loosened up brushstroke, and flattened form to create moody, nearly crepuscular effects. *Etretat*, done in 1875, remains relatively naturalistic, although we notice a free brushstroke, a somewhat cursory description of detail, and an interest in creating atmosphere. We are drawn into the scene by a path in the verdant, pastoral foreground that wends its way through a village, indicated by rooftops and puffing chimneys, toward the cliffs and shore. A solid horizontal register of light to dark blues defines the sea, and an admixture of inky blues and azures, punctuated by the gritty whites of the clouds, constitutes the sky. Thus, greens and blues encircle the greyish-white of the cliffs. The painting suggests Inness's exposure to French art, particularly the Barbizon school, the work of Camille Corot, and perhaps even Impressionism. But as *Etretat* demonstrates, Impressionism for Inness meant mood and sentiment rather than pure perception and optics.

163

JAMES ABBOTT MCNEILL WHISTLER

b. Lowell, Massachusetts, 1834
d. London, 1903

Coast of Brittany: Alone with the Tide

1861
Oil on canvas
87.2 x 115.7 cm. (34 5/16 x 45 9/16 in.)
In memory of William Arnold Healy,
    given by his daughter Susie
    Healy Camp
Acquisition no. 1925.393

When asked to describe his art, James McNeill Whistler replied, "It is an arrangement of line, form and colour first." That Whistler was most concerned with composition in his work is attested to throughout his career. In this context, it is worth mentioning that his famous popularized piece commonly known as "Whistler's Mother" was actually titled *Arrangement in Gray and Black No. 1: The Artist's Mother*: obviously, pictorial rather than filial instincts came first.

Born in the United States, Whistler travelled extensively. He eventually settled in England, where his work achieved great acclaim. A superb portraitist and skilled painter of landscape, Whistler's art is best characterized by its refinement. Harmonies of wan colors, applied with thin washes of paint, are arranged in a relatively flat, simplified, decorative manner. This extreme refinement led to rarefaction and even decadence and Whistler, influenced by Symbolism and by Oriental art, favored exoticism and an art of nuance.

In the late 1850s, Whistler lived in France, where he made contact with Courbet, Baudelaire, and Manet. After his work was rejected by the Salon on several occasions, he grew closer to the French avant garde and participated in the famous Salon des Refuses of 1863. *Coast of Brittany: Alone with the Tide* was done while on a trip to a part of the French coast that was becoming increasingly attractive to artists.

This canvas comes from a somewhat individual period in Whistler's art, when his pigment is more impastoed and his colors more hearty. This ruggedness is generally attributed to the influence of Courbet, but it should be pointed out that Courbet's gruff landscapes date primarily from the mid-1860s. In any event, Whistler's penchant for tonal harmonies, limited color contrasts, and flat horizontal zones of color is evident here.

Later in his career, Whistler's preoccupation with purely formal arrangement led to John Ruskin's charge that the artist was "flinging a pot of paint in the public's face." How often have we heard similar invective directed against ground-breaking art?

JOHN SINGER SARGENT

b. Florence, 1856
d. London, 1925

Ruth Sears Bacon

1887
Oil on canvas
123.8 x 92.1 cm. (48 3/4 x 36 1/4 in.)
Gift of Mrs. Austin Cheney
Acquisition no. 1975.92

John Singer Sargent was once described as "an American born in Italy, educated in France, who looks like a German, and paints like a Spaniard." An international man, whose urbanity informed his art, Sargent was a most wanted portrait painter of the world's aristocracy. His popularity stemmed from his flashy technique, which flattered his sitters. As a result, Sargent's reputation has waned and waxed; to some individuals and generations, he was a brilliant technician whose best works are masterful compositions that frequently capture the psychology of his sitters; to others, he was an often superficial showman, who knew how to puff personality, not penetrate it.

This portrait of *Ruth Sears Bacon* aptly illustrates Sargent's pyrotechnic handling of paint. Seated on a chair covered with sheets, the young child actually appears adrift in a sea of paint. Her face, which seems to withhold rather than offer information, is the only carefully finished area, and it stands out strangely amidst this riotous fluff of pigment. This is the Sargent whose facility and fluency had become a mannerism in late nineteenth-century stylish portraiture, not the brilliant composer of the famous *Daughters of Edward Darley Boit* or the exposer of upper-class values in the notorious *Madame X*. Still, his bravura brush, culled from the art of Velázquez, Hals, and Manet, and his creamy whip of colors, from sugary whites to confectionary blues, accented by dashes of black and cordovan, provide their own delights.

166

167

THOMAS DEWING

b. Boston, 1851
d. New York, 1938

The Days

1887
Oil on canvas
109.7 x 182.9 cm. (43 3/16 x 72 in.)
Gift from the Estates of Louise
    Cheney and Anne W. Cheney
Acquisition no. 1944.328

The work of Thomas Dewing captures a certain mood characteristic of the late nineteenth century. His primary subject was the idealized female, represented either in intimate, domestic interiors or in vaporous, wistful landscapes. Refined and elegant in the extreme, these works are part of a *fin-de-siècle* aestheticism, with its attendant sense of malaise. In a world in which revolutions in science, technology, and psychology effected a shift in values, certain artists, writers, and poets, clinging to the beliefs of an earlier age, concomitantly expressed nostalgia for a bygone era and a sense of disenchantment, even alienation, within contemporary life.

That women were often the icons of this sensibility results from the significance of their changing role in society. The new woman—increasingly liberated, fighting for the vote, sexually less inhibited, patron of avant-garde art, emancipator of traditional dance and theater, is ignored in Dewing's art. His females are innocent, virginal, ideal or domesticated, ensconced in atmospheric landscapes or in the "gilded cage" of the home. He represents an image of woman fading fast in the face of a new generation.

Dewing's *The Days* of 1887 reflects this nostalgia, with a chorus of women arranged almost frieze-like in one of his dewy landscapes. Tucked into the dense space of a verdant arcadia, the ladies hold objects such as musical instruments, specifically ones that produce soft, melodious tones and carry associations with the orphic world of an earlier time. A fan is his requisite hommage to Orientalism, and the figures are dressed in gauzy tunics harking back to the antique. The women are carefully delineated, substantiating Dewing's reputation as a superb draftsman. The origins of this linearity in the work of artists like Botticelli, along with the compendium of pastoral motifs, also suggest that Dewing shared similar sources and interests with the Pre-Raphaelites. The close-valued palette of the piece is exemplary of the late nineteenth-century tonalism of artists like Whistler, and its predominant pale blue-green cast was common to many of Dewing's paintings.

WILLIAM H. HARNETT

b. Clonakilty, Ireland, 1848
d. New York, 1892

The Faithful Colt

1890
Oil on canvas
57.2 x 47 cm. (22 1/2 x 19 in.)
The Ella Gallup Sumner and Mary
   Catlin Sumner Collection
Acquisition no. 1935.236

ELI WHITNEY, JR.

b. 1820
d. 1895

Army Holster Pistol

1847
9-inch barrel (22.9 cm.)
The Elizabeth Hart Jarvis Colt
   Collection
Acquisition no. 1905.988

The Wadsworth Atheneum's *The Faithful Colt* by William M. Harnett is an extraordinary work of art with a remarkable history. Initially regarded as a typical piece of American folk painting, *The Faithful Colt* was rediscovered at the Downtown Gallery of New York in 1935 by Edith Halpert, who in turn sold it to the Wadsworth Atheneum that same year. The piece struck curators as so stunningly accomplished that the search was on for more works by the relatively unknown Harnett. With time, more pieces surfaced, resulting in the first modern exhibition of Harnett's art, in 1939. Since then, Harnett's reputation has grown and more information about his life and work has been gathered.

What is most mesmerizing about Harnett's art is its *trompe l'oeil* quality. *Trompe l'oeil* means "fool the eye," a term used to describe works of such striking verisimilitude that they can be confused with reality itself. Harnett's main motif was still life, and *The Faithful Colt* is typical of his formats. The background of the painting simulates a wall on which several objects hang. Because the space of the work is so shallow and its ground so nearly contiguous with the wall on which the painting itself sits, the attached objects exert a powerful three-dimensional pressure. Here, on weathered, dark green planks, studded with cracks, grooves, splinters, stains, and rusty nails, a pistol is pegged, and it, too, is a technical tour de force, with its cracked ivory handle, rusted, hammered barrel, and delicately textured brass fittings. A legible newspaper clipping, slightly crinkled, seems glued to the boards, and, so as not to disrupt the persuasiveness of its illusion, Harnett makes his signature appear as graffito etched into the wood.

It has been argued that the kind of obsession with ultraclarity and superrealism found in Harnett's work is endemic to American art, symptomatic of the country's materialism, pragmatism, and love of the tangible. Certainly, *trompe l'oeil* characteristics can be found among America's pioneer painters, such as John Singleton Copley and Raphaelle Peale, and continue up to the present day in the work of the Pop and Photo-Realist artists, but to isolate such a characteristic as distinctly American seems somewhat tendentious.

The subject of Harnett's painting, a Colt pistol, is particularly suited to the Wadsworth Atheneum. Elizabeth Hart Jarvis Colt, the wife of Samuel Colt and a great benefactor of the museum, donated, among other bequests, her husband's outstanding collection of firearms. The collection is significant in that it includes wooden prototypes of the guns manufactured by Colt in Hartford. The present example is an army holster pistol made by Eli Whitney, Jr. for Samuel Colt.

JULIUS STEWART

b. Philadelphia, 1855
d. Paris, 1919

The Yacht "Namouna" in Venetian Waters

1890
Oil on canvas
142.2 x 195.6 cm. (56 x 77 in.)
The Ella Gallup Sumner and
  Mary Catlin Sumner Collection
Acquisition no. 1965.32

Born in Philadelphia, Julius Stewart spent most of his life in Paris. He studied in France with the great academician Jean-Leon Gérôme, from whom he learned a form of academic classicism that stressed carefully plotted perspective spaces, smooth finish, scrupulous detail, sculptural roundness of form—all in all, a kind of beautiful ultra-realism, which so approached the realm of the ideal that his portrayals can seem artificial and airless.

Stewart plied his painterly wares in Parisian high society, and he became a sought-after painter of the urbane, fashionable life of the continent. In addition, he produced a number of idealized female nudes located in outdoor settings, and these figures have the somewhat bloodless beauty, proportion, and porcelain finish of nineteenth-century academic sculpture.

The Yacht "Namouna" in Venetian Waters is one of his sophisticated, modish scenes. It portrays an outing on the Adriatic in the luxurious yacht Namouna, owned by newspaper baron James Gordon Bennett (in the white suit), and his guests, including the famous actress and socialite Lily Langtry (in the wicker chair). These wealthy, handsome, and flirtatious figures are captured in infinite detail, but it is exactly these qualities of precision and perfection that create a latent sense of ennui. Other elements in the work also appear disturbing. Action is frozen by super-clarity. The viewpoint accentuating the tilt of the boat and the disconnected arrangement of the figures create instability, even tension. Bright sunlight penetrates the scene in only a few small patches; placed under a protective canopy, the figures are bathed in a more even light that further promotes a sense of stillness. Reminiscent of some of the work of James Tissot and Gustave Caillebotte, the art of Julius Stewart may also indicate the influence of the camera, particularly in the zooming space found in wide-angle photography.

WILLIAM MERRITT CHASE

b. Williamsburg, Indiana, 1849
d. New York, 1916

Boy Smoking (The Apprentice)

1875
Oil on canvas
94.1 x 58.4 cm. (37 1/16 x 23 in.)
J. J. Goodwin Fund
Acquisition no. 1927.169

After a brief art training in America, William Merritt Chase so impressed some art patrons in St. Louis that they offered him support to study in Europe. When presented with this opportunity, Chase summarized the aspirations of a whole generation of American artists by replying, "I'd rather go to Europe than go to Heaven." Most artists travelled to England, France, or possibly Italy. It is significant that Chase selected Munich, where the current style looked back to the animate art of seventeenth-century Holland. The bravura brush and dramatically spontaneous approach of Frans Hals was a key inspiration. As a result, Chase adopted this loose and dashing style and applied it to a wide range of subjects, including portraiture, genre, and landscape.

Boy Smoking (The Apprentice) consists of noticeable brushstrokes that impart a sense of spontaneity to this genre portrait. The work strongly recalls Frans Hals's portrayals of lively figures. The dark tonalities of the background and of the boy's overalls are contrasted with the brighter hues of flesh, shirt, hair, and bandana. Later in his career, Chase lightened his palette and loosened his stroke further, probably under the influence of French Impressionism and the works of Sargent, Velázquez, and Whistler.

Bravura brushstroke became the fashionable style in late nineteenth-century America, and Chase was one of its most successful practitioners. He also became a famous teacher, taking on private pupils at his Tenth Street studio, and eventually established the Chase School in New York in 1896. Continuing to exalt the liberated brush, Chase influenced an entire generation of American artists. A talented and witty teacher, Chase once advised his students: "Take plenty of time for your picture. Take two hours if you need it."

175

THOMAS EAKINS

b. Philadelphia, 1844
d. Philadelphia, 1916

John McLure Hamilton

1895
Oil on canvas
203.2 x 127.7 cm. (80 x 50 1/4 in.)
The Ella Gallup Sumner and
    Mary Catlin Sumner Collection
Acquisition no. 1947.399

Painter, sculptor, and photographer, Thomas Eakins was one of America's foremost realist artists. His interest in science, mathematics, and medicine informed his art: he painted scrupulously observed scenes of doctors at work and figures and animals in motion, with compositions plotted out according to rigorous perspective systems.

Eakins was also a superb portraitist, as is illustrated by his depiction of John McLure Hamilton, who was also a portrait painter. By placing a full-length figure against an undefined background (a procedure he adopted after seeing the works of Velázquez in Spain), Eakins focuses complete attention on the body. Though the stance of the figure is confident, the soft greys and browns of the trousers and jacket fuse with similar hues in the background. In contrast, brows and eyes are highlighted; thus, Eakins indicates that the power of the artist lies in his thoughts and vision. Devoid of puffery and trappings, this sober portrait accentuates the central role of man's mind. Herein lies Eakins's uniqueness as an artist. For him, psychology and intellect, not material goods, were paramount. Painted before Sigmund Freud formulated his theories on personality, this work presents a pictorial thesis emphasizing the power of the mind. The Hamilton portrait, like other of Eakins's solitary figures, augurs that peculiarly twentieth-century affliction, alienation.

JOHN SLOAN

b. Lockhaven, Pennsylvania, 1871
d. Hanover, New Hampshire, 1951

Hairdresser's Window

1907
Oil on canvas
81 x 66 cm. (31 $^7/_8$ x 26 in.)
The Ella Gallup Sumner and
   Mary Catlin Sumner Collection
Acquisition no. 1947.240

John Sloan's *Hairdresser's Window* personifies the emergence of a new kind of art in America in the early twentieth century. Labelled "Ashcan" painting by contemptuous critics, this work focused on the often unheroic human interactions of the contemporary urbanscape. The challenge of this new style came during a period when the National Academy of Design, the organization of the ruling artistic elite, still prescribed that the role of art was to improve upon nature. The Academy insisted that artists select only edifying subjects such as mythology, history, or religion and that the inhabitants of these works possess beauty to rival that of classical gods. Since it also controlled the selection and display of art at major exhibitions, those artists who failed to meet Academic standards had difficulty finding an audience.

Just as President Teddy Roosevelt had attempted to break up corporate monopolies, Ashcan artists sought to ease the aesthetic stranglehold of the Academy. They organized alternative exhibitions where their antiestablishment art was shown. As in Sloan's *Hairdresser's Window*, many of these works dealt with the activities of daily life. Trained as a newspaper illustrator, Sloan employed a similarly sketchy style in his paintings to impart a sense of the captured moment. He did not, however, ignore pictorial structure, for *Hairdresser's Window* is organized by a series of rectangular shapes, placed parallel to the picture plane, with the curves of the figures functioning as foils in the shallow space of the piece. Sloan was affiliated with several socialist causes, and his concentration on the common man expresses his humanitarian sympathies.

178

179

MARSDEN HARTLEY

b. Lewiston, Maine, 1877
d. Ellsworth, Maine, 1943

Military

1913
Oil on canvas
99.7 x 99.7 cm. (39 1/4 x 39 1/4 in.)
The Ella Gallup Sumner and
   Mary Catlin Sumner Collection
Acquisition no. 1973.2

Paintings of war and the military often express the heroics of its fighters. Yet, the genuine psychology behind modern warfare is to transform the act of killing and wounding into a deed done in the service of an ideal. Thus, the combatant is made to believe he is fighting for a cause, not committing murder. The American artist Marsden Hartley understood this goal: his numerous paintings of military themes, done in Berlin in the early and mid-teens, emphasize the symbols of war—its pageantry, medals, uniforms, flag-waving—rather than death and destruction. The trappings of war, with their attendant machismo, also held appeal for the homosexual Hartley, and while in Berlin he had an affair with both a fellow artist and a German lieutenant. As Hartley himself described it, he "lived rather gaily in the Berlin fashion—with all that implies."

Military of 1913 is an illustrative work of the period. Executed in Berlin, it contains an array of forms, many of which are unidentifiable. Images of numbers dominate, referring to the mathematical precision essential to the military mentality. With its bright yet sooty colors, this dynamic, nearly abstract work was probably inspired by Kandinsky's animate abstractions of landscapes, and it evokes the activity and dash of the military.

The elevation of numbers to key components of the work reaffirms contemporary Cubist experiments with numbers and letters in art. But while in Cubism letters and numbers, often yanked out of context and thrust into a work, suggest that they, like the more conventional elements of a work of art, are nothing more than symbols, Hartley wished to maintain the associative power of numbers both because of their links to military operations and their potential mysticism.

With the advent of World War II, Hartley returned to the United States. His art underwent several stylistic changes, and he eventually arrived at a crude, intentionally awkward style of brooding, yet agitated landscape images.

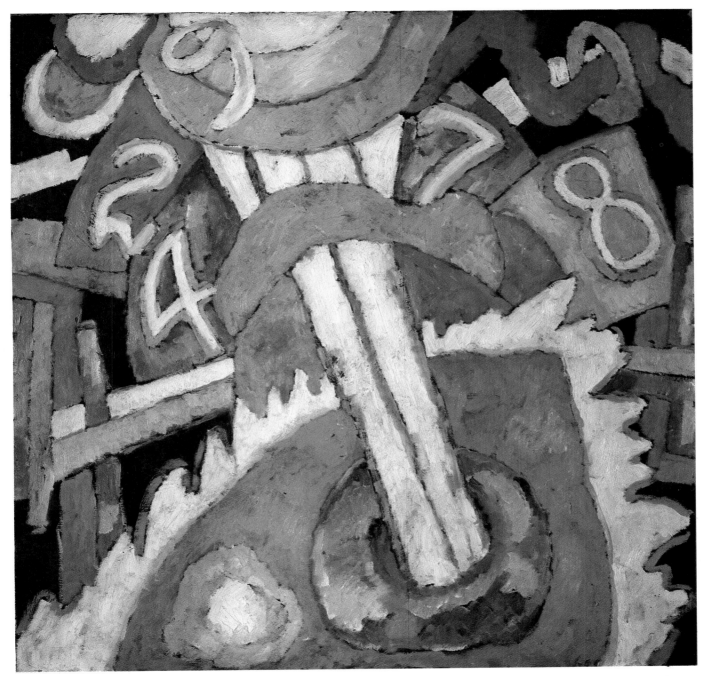

181

GEORGIA O'KEEFFE

b. Sun Prairie, Wisconsin, 1887

The Lawrence Tree

1929
Oil on canvas
78.7 x 99.1 cm. (31 x 39 in.)
The Ella Gallup Sumner and
    Mary Catlin Sumner Collection
Acquisition no. 1981.23

Georgia O'Keeffe, like other American artists such as Arthur Dove and Edward Steichen, perceived the world in a fashion that emphasized formal qualities. In the mid-teens of this century, she pioneered a remarkably radical form of nature-oriented abstraction. As a student of Arthur Wesley Dow, she was instructed in the importance of the decorative in painting, an idea that Dow had discovered in Oriental art. O'Keeffe's contact with Alfred Stieglitz, the owner of the *291* gallery who later became her husband, provided her with numerous stimuli. Through Stieglitz, she became acquainted with photography, and at *291* she undoubtedly saw avant-garde photographic work that transformed everyday objects into forceful abstractions. Purification and reduction as paths toward the abstract could also have been acquired from other work shown at *291,* including African art and Brancusi's sculptures.

Nature was O'Keeffe's primary inspiration. *The Lawrence Tree,* a nocturnal scene executed in Taos in 1929, aptly demonstrates her approach. O'Keeffe presents the subject from below, producing a tension between the depth of the drastically foreshortened tree and the flatness asserted by insistent shapes, purged of most interior modelling. Although objects have become less recognizable, they often reveal an inner life, because their organic and sinuous shapes evoke processes of growth and the fecundity of nature. Here, the forms are highly suggestive, as blurred edges and suffused colors create a magical atmosphere.

Living in New Mexico, O'Keeffe remains one of America's finest artists; from the teens through today, her unique vision of nature has continued to be inspirational.

STANTON MACDONALD-WRIGHT

b. Charlottesville, Virginia, 1890
d. Pacific Palisades, California, 1973

American Synchromy No. 1

Ca. 1919
Oil on canvas
87 x 58.4 cm. (34 1/4 x 23 in.)
The Ella Gallup Sumner and
   Mary Catlin Sumner Collection
Acquisition no. 1971.77

As an aspiring American artist, Stanton Macdonald-Wright made the trip to Paris obligatory in the early twentieth century, in order to work and study. There, he teamed with another temporary expatriate, Morgan Russell, to found a new art movement. Officially launching their invention with an exhibition in Munich in 1913, Wright and Russell called this novel style Synchromism, which means "with color." The frequently purely abstract work of the duo was but one of many experiments in color abstraction being carried out in Europe and America at the time; among others were the art of Robert Delaunay, Fernand Léger, František Kupka, Giacomo Balla, Wassily Kandinsky, Augusto Giacometti, and Arthur Dove.

The goal of Synchromism was to arrange planes of color and light that would create compositional syncopations of a purely abstract nature while they also evoked a sense of three-dimensional form. The Synchromists' greatest stimulus came from Cézanne, who pioneered the related technique of employing patches of color so as to produce both independent pictorial structure and fidelity to the observed motif.

Moreover, the term Synchromy carries musical connotations. During a period when visual artists were first exploring abstraction, they looked to music, an inherently abstract medium, as a model. This interest in synesthesia involved both visual artists and musicians: for example, artists assigned colors to sounds and attempted to create chromatic equivalents of aural harmonies; at the same time, musicians also formulated color-sound equations and, in a forerunner to the modern light show, programmed colored lights to glow in accompaniment to musical performances.

Stanton Macdonald-Wright's American Synchromy No. 1 was done after Wright returned to America in 1916, at which time Synchromist ideas became fairly influential on numerous American modernists. Part of a generally conservative current in postwar art, this particular piece suggests a retrenchment from the more abstract and concrete synchromist canvases of the movement's heyday in the early and mid-teens. Here, a twisting figure, most likely based on a work of Michelangelo (a common source for Wright and Russell), is clearly recognizable, and its spectrum of colors also functions as conventional darker modelling, defining the musculature and contours of the lighter-toned figure.

185

ELIE NADELMAN

b. Warsaw, 1885
d. Riverdale, New York, 1946

Dancer

1918
Painted cherry wood
71.8 cm. high (28 1/4 in.)
The Philip L. Goodwin Collection
Acquisition no. 1958.224

Throughout his career, Elie Nadelman was strongly attracted to folk and primitive art and to the qualities of geometric reduction or volumetric stylization in modernist sculpture. In Europe, he drew inspiration from sources as diverse as antique dolls, Greek archaic sculpture, and the work of Picasso and Brancusi. After arriving in America during the war, in 1914, he was exposed to American folk art, the purity and naivety of which amplified his belief in the expressive potential of the simplified sculptural statement.

Dancer dates from 1918, the period during which American folk art first exerted its charms on Nadelman. With exposure to folk art, Nadelman began working with wood, which he later painted, continuing his involvement with sculpture created by direct carving rather than by an additive process. He was originally inspired in this way by Greek statuary and Brancusi's pieces. The polished surfaces and curvilinear volumes of his art may owe something to Brancusi, but his early training as a draftsman in the Art Nouveau style is also revealed here. Terpsichorean themes were particularly popular in America at the time, including the many portrayals of the radical American dancer Isadora Duncan. But there is something of the can-can girl in Nadelman's twisting high-kicking figure and something also of the stylized linear rhythms of Georges Seurat, an artist whom Nadelman admired.

Though they are modest works, Nadelman's suave, elegant, and witty concoctions of slightly puffy, almost rubbery volumes are among the relatively rare examples of genuine modern sculpture in America early in the century. In their evocation of the American folk tradition, they also offer a beguiling variation of the modernist obsession with primitive art.

FLORINE STETTHEIMER

b. Rochester, New York, 1871 (?)
d. New York, 1944

Beauty Contest: To the Memory of P.T. Barnum

1924
Oil on canvas
127 x 153 cm. (50 x 60 1/4 in.)
Gift of Miss Ettie Stettheimer
Acquisition no. 1947.242

The art of Florine Stettheimer is both odd and charming. While its inhabitants constitute the bohemian and sophisticated avant garde of America, they are portrayed in a self-consciously naive fashion. Without question, there is something of the caricature in Stettheimer's paintings, with their curvilinearly described, marionette-like figures. These paper-thin, svelte, and attenuated individuals occupy an ethereal and rarefied space made even more hermetic by sugary white backgrounds and other confectionary hues.

Suggestive of a cross between a wedding cake and a pinball machine, *Beauty Contest: To the Memory of P. T. Barnum* contains a partly recognizable cast of characters enlisted from the artist's circle of friends, consisting mainly of artists, performers, and intellectuals. Florine herself appears in the upper left, wearing a magenta gown with hair color to match. Beside her is Edward Steichen, the photographer, whose shooting of the beauty pageant most likely alludes to his involvement at the time with fashion photography. Other possible identifications include Rudolph Valentino at the lower center of the composition, P. T. Barnum, the white-haired gentleman standing at the right, and Carl van Vechten at the typewriter. (See Ann Sutherland Harris and Linda Nochlin, *Women Artists: 1550–1950*, Los Angeles County Museum, 1976, p. 267.) It has even been suggested that the slinky contestants are more transvestite than flapper, and that we are witness to a "Harlem Drag Ball," appropriate to Stettheimer's satiric inclinations. Referring to a subject she found both amusing and grotesque, she once remarked, "Beauty contests are a B.L.O.T. on American something—I believe life—or civilization." In this context, Stettheimer's sensibility borders on "camp," that affectation and posture derived from late nineteenth-century dandyism and continuing on in present-day Pop.

Florine Stettheimer, although private and aloof, organized a leading New York salon, counting among its visitors Alfred Stieglitz, Charles Demuth, Edward Steichen, Elie Nadelman, Henry McBride, Marcel Duchamp, Gaston Lachaise, and Albert Gleizes, many of whom make cameo appearances in her art. She wrote poetry and designed the sets and costumes for the Gertrude Stein-Virgil Thompson opera *Four Saints in Three Acts*, which premiered at the Wadsworth Atheneum in 1934.

189

RAPHAEL SOYER

b. Tombou, Russia, 1899

Sixth Avenue

Ca. 1930–34
Oil on canvas
66.3 x 81.6 cm. (26 1/8 x 32 1/8 in.)
Gift of Mr. and Mrs.
  James N. Rosenberg
Acquisition no. 1947.18

One of the major developments in American art during the 1930s was the emergence of "American Scene" painting. "American Scene" art is representational work in which native American life was the primary subject. It had two main divisions: the first was Regionalism, a politically conservative circle including Thomas Hart Benton, John Steuart Curry, and Grant Wood, who exalted traditional American values and chronicled American small-town and rural life; the second was the more radical, somewhat socialist-oriented Urban or Social Realism, consisting of such artists as Ben Shahn, William Gropper, Reginald Marsh, and Raphael Soyer, who helped to inspire reformist sympathies, frequently through depictions of urban squalor. Undoubtedly, this deep interest in indigenous America was spurred by the Depression, which so shook the foundations of the country that artists, along with writers, sociologists, and political theorists, undertook serious investigations of fundamental American values and roots. This exploration was, in fact, encouraged by the government itself, since many of the federally sponsored art projects directed artists toward nearly archaeological documentation of autochthonous American life and artifacts.

Raphael Soyer was a Russian immigrant who, upon arriving in America, worked odd jobs during the day to pay for art school at night. A humanitarian artist, he developed a representational style that took as its model the work of some of the great realist artists of the past, including Goya, Eakins, Homer, and Degas. Soyer's art of the thirties, the period of his greatest popularity, is exemplary of Urban Realism. *Sixth Avenue* is typical of his art: the main subject matter is lower-class workers, the impoverished, and the dispossessed. Grim figures inhabit less than cheery surroundings, and frequently paint is scumbled and color is somber and brooding. The tragic mood of *Sixth Avenue* is intensified by the cropping of the figures, who are packed into the front plane of the piece and placed in a shallow space, suggesting an inability to escape their fate. Soyer, one of three brother artists, not only recorded the condition of others but also diaristically explored himself in one of the largest series of self-portraits within the history of American art.

STUART DAVIS

b. Philadelphia, 1894
d. New York, 1964

Midi

1954
Oil on canvas
71.1 x 92 cm. (28 x 36 3/16 in.)
The Henry Schnakenberg Fund
Acquisition no. 1954.56

One of Stuart Davis's major achievements was to take three key modern European developments—Cubism, Fauvism, and Futurism—and apply them to the expression of distinctively American subjects. He even uses a French appellation, *Midi*, for a painting that portrays the Yankee city of Gloucester, Massachusetts. From Cubism, Davis borrowed the technique of fragmenting forms and rearranging them in his canvas for the sake of pictorial balance and construction. From Fauvism, he learned the expressive potential of flat, sometimes strident hues, interlocked in a decorative arrangement across the canvas surface. And finally, from Futurism, he understood the power of thrusting disparate moments and locales into a single work so that the pandemonium and simultaneity of modern life might be evoked.

What Davis also knew was that these European styles were well suited to the qualities of the American landscape, particularly to cities and roadside architecture. It is this dialogue between high art and vernacular forms that gives his work such tremendous vitality. *Midi* of 1954, for example, based on sketches the artist made of the Gloucester waterfront many years earlier, is a characteristic Davis piece, in which the interaction of flat, vibrantly colored, jigsaw-puzzle-like forms creates jazzy syncopations and vivid pulsations. A hot magenta background plays host to a wide range of hard-edged green, white, blue, black, and orange color shapes. Davis's zinging colors, flat space, sharp-edged forms, and interest in the contemporary visual environment also anticipate some of the concerns of two later major developments of the 1960s: Pop art and Color-field Painting.

193

MILTON AVERY

b. Altmar, New York, 1893
d. New York, 1965

Husband and Wife

1945
Oil on canvas
85.7 x 111.8 cm (33 3/4 x 44 in.)
Gift of Mr. and Mrs.
 Roy R. Neuberger
Acquisition no. 1955.142

Milton Avery occupies a unique position in American art of the twentieth century. Though not a purely abstract artist, he nevertheless influenced some of America's foremost abstract painters, including Mark Rothko and Adolph Gottlieb. This was the result of Avery's ability to transform a motif into a basically flat, economical arrangement of interlocking color shapes, from which all inessential details were eliminated. The lyrical harmonies achieved through these interwedged blocks of colors are what most impressed the American Color-field artists, and these connections between Avery and the abstractionists force us to reconsider the relationship between supposed non-representational, "formalist" art and subjects derived from nature.

Husband and Wife demonstrates Avery's translation of a motif into art. Individual objects are purged of the extraneous, except for the occasional contours created by canals of white canvas. Each object is assigned a sweet color, and the combination of these hues often produces surprising and charming effects. Mostly flat and decorative, the work has a slight elliptical bulge of form beginning at the lower left center and arching up both sides, with space becoming deeper on the right. Initially, the scene seems typical of Avery: he preferred calm, leisurely portrayals of landscapes, figures, and domesticity. As is often the case in his art, there is a witty ungainliness to his forms and a beguiling quirkiness to his contours, which add a touch of humor to his intimate scenes. However, all may not be tranquil here. We are witness, apparently, to a conversation in which the husband seems to be making a point and the wife seems unconvinced, or perhaps mildly annoyed. Moreover, this speculation about the subject of Husband and Wife suggests that Avery assigned colors to forms with more than the decorative in mind, as is manifested here in the hues of the couple's respective faces: fiery crimson for the man's, sour green for the woman's.

194

195

ANDREW WYETH

b. Chadds Ford, Pennsylvania, 1917

Chambered Nautilus

1956
Tempera on masonite
62.9 x 122.5 cm. (24 3/4 x 48 1/4 in.)
From the Collection of Mr. and Mrs.
   Robert Montgomery
Acquisition no. 1979.168

Andrew Wyeth is a curious phenomenon in the art world. Probably the most popular artist in America, he is sometimes omitted in so-called serious surveys of modern art. The first artist ever to grace the cover of *Time* magazine, he is also the first living painter to receive a major retrospective at the Metropolitan Museum of Art. Certain scholars have condemned Wyeth for clinging to realism in the midst of an era characterized primarily by abstraction. But so much of the best radical, avant-garde art is representational in origin or nature that this criticism seems beside the point. What also disturbs critics is Wyeth's penchant for sentiment, that is, his willingness to play upon our emotions. Moreover, it is argued that his nostalgia for a bygone era and his homespun themes smack of a conservatism that has reactionary social implications.

In all fairness to Wyeth, it is best to dispense with the polemic and simply examine one of his images. In the case of *Chambered Nautilus*, we have the paradigmatic Wyeth subject of a cripple or pariah who struggles against his or her handicap. The figure is Merle James, Wyeth's mother-in-law, a nearly bedridden invalid. Wyeth portrays her in bed, staring wistfully out her window at the sea. Near her sits a straw basket, and at the foot of the bed is the chambered nautilus of the title of the piece. The basket contains a Bible, which is probably meant to imply her faith in the immortality of the spirit within her withering, mortal, bodily shell.

There is no denying the technical skill of Wyeth in this work. He has used egg tempera as his medium in order to achieve the meticulousness, dryness, and subtlety characteristic of his best art. Typically, this piece is composed of muted beige tones, from an outer ring of sepia shades to a variety of off-whites describing the hazy, glaring light coming in the window. Furthermore, the work is constructed in shallow parallel planes with the elements of the canopied four-poster and the rectangularly divided window creating a solid, framing armature for the piece. Its tightness and muteness create a wistful, tragic air, and herein lies Wyeth's greatest strength. The melancholy ambiance is seductive, but problems can arise from it because such scenes are prone to appear anecdotal and overly sentimental.

JOSEPH CORNELL

b. Nyack, New York, 1903
d. Flushing, New York, 1972

Soap Bubble Set

1936
Construction
40 x 36.2 x 13.7 cm. (15 3/4 x 14 1/4 x
    5 7/16 in.)
The Henry and Walker Keney Fund
Acquisition no. 1938.270

Joseph Cornell is one of America's most idiosyncratic artists. Something of a recluse, he spent most of his time in his house on Utopia Parkway in Flushing, New York, creating little "Utopian" worlds in his art. Inspired by the Surrealist belief that unusual juxtapositions create visual poetry, Cornell specialized in filling small "shadow boxes" with a variety of common and unusual objects. His act of sealing artifacts in hermetic environments was akin to that of the conservationist or museologist. His preservations were symbolic of his efforts to protect the ephemera of the past, particularly the Romantic and Symbolist past which he idolized, from the ravages of time.

Soap Bubble Set personifies Cornell's conservational concerns. A worn, brown wood box, covered with glass and fitted with metal handles, is divided into seven main compartments. The central zone contains an antique French map of the moon, and other planetary allusions include two images of Saturn, one rising above a Renaissance townscape, the other encircling an equestrian statue. The presence of the clay pipe, out of which the moon map seems to sprout, accounts for the title *Soap Bubble Set.*

The Wadsworth Atheneum's piece may well be the first of what was to be a fruitful series of similarly classified works. Cornell has mentioned that soap bubble pipes reminded him of his childhood, and we see that, once again, memory and the effort to preserve the past are critical to his art. Reminiscences of childhood are further evoked in the pedestalled doll's head. Moreover, Cornell's mini-worlds, with their own structure and rules, should remind us of games, those of childhood and otherwise, in which fantasy and "counter-reality" are key components. Here, the pipe gives birth to the moon, suggesting not only otherworldliness but also an association with night and the realm of dreams. Like soap bubbles themselves, perfect little spheres, fragile and exquisite, Cornell creates ideal worlds, freezing them in time and space. The egg in a cordial glass reemphasizes the theme of fragility, while further referring to the birth of an idea (his first "Soap Bubble" piece) and the birth of a cosmos.

CARTE GÉOGRAPHIQUE DE LA LUNE

ROBERT RAUSCHENBERG

b. Port Arthur, Texas, 1925

Retroactive I

1964
Oil and silkscreen ink on canvas
213.4 x 152.4 cm. (84 x 60 in.)
Gift of Susan Morse Hilles
Acquisition no. 1964.30

Robert Rauschenberg, along with the artist Jasper Johns, effected a major change in the direction of contemporary American art in the 1950s and 1960s. Since the late 1940s, Abstract Expressionism had been the reigning movement; it emphasized the metaphysical power of abstraction (though it was not exclusively non-objective art) and presented the artistic process as evidence of profound emotions such as existential anxiety. Rauschenberg saw nothing particularly sacrosanct in either pure abstraction or pure gesturalism. Thus, he reintroduced recognizable imagery into art, often by attaching real objects to the work. The images were mostly mundane, and Rauschenberg preferred the popular icons of contemporary mass media, such as newspapers, magazines, and television. Among these were advertisements, comic strips, photos of political figures, and reproductions of famous masterpieces. Thus, in a single work, a picture of the Sistine ceiling might cohabit with a Sunkist Oranges ad, a photo of the Statue of Liberty, the image of a stuffed bird, and slashes of paint. When real objects were included, his works, now called "combines," grew in size, sometimes approaching the scale of a total environment.

Rauschenberg's art is indebted to the earlier tradition of collage and Dada, particularly the work of Kurt Schwitters, but his preoccupation with geometric regularity probably derives from Josef Albers, who was his teacher at Black Mountain College. *Retroactive I*, while not literally a collage, is a mélange of elements, including a fruit ad, a parachutist, a nude descending a staircase (a reference to the famous work by Marcel Duchamp), paint drips and a picture of President John F. Kennedy. Rauschenberg was fascinated by Kennedy: here he selects a drawing of the President delivering a speech on television, which triggers associations with Kennedy's unique oratory, which was often punctuated by the kind of hand gestures that the artist represents twice. Rauschenberg helped to shift American art away from Abstract Expressionism, and to propel it toward Pop Art through his use of popular, media-derived imagery.

WILLEM DE KOONING

b. Rotterdam, 1904

Montauk I

1969
Oil on canvas
123.5 x 195.6 cm. (48 5/8 x 77 in.)
The Ella Gallup Sumner and
    Mary Catlin Sumner Collection
Acquisition no. 1973.46

Willem de Kooning is one of America's most vital artists. His career often alternates between periods of figuration and abstraction. For example, after a remarkable series of urban-oriented, predominantly black-and-white abstractions of the late 1940s and early 1950s, he produced his most famous series of paintings of women in the early 1950s. On large canvases, de Kooning applied massive, slashing slabs of fat paint to portray images of women. The physicality of approach often makes the figures appear threatening. Big-busted, long-legged, with leering eyes and glistening, sinister smiles, these women are de Kooning's modern-day equivalent to the bulky madonnas of Italian Gothic and early Renaissance art; but now the model is the fifties woman of advertising and pinups (such as Marilyn Monroe). These paintings often express the artist's conception of the duality of woman as concomitantly enticing and menacing, a kind of Madonna-Aphrodite hybrid. Moreover, de Kooning's style became a trademark of Abstract Expressionism, because his exaltation of the artistic process was seen as a revelation of the individual's inner feelings.

Initially, the center of Abstract Expressionism was New York City. However, de Kooning, like several others in his circle, began in the early 1950s to spend time on the eastern tip of Long Island. Eventually, in 1961, he moved permanently to the Springs, in Easthampton, and this area has since become a chic mecca for artists and intellectuals. This shift in locale brought about an alteration in his art. While women still inhabit his environments, the ladies diminish in substance, and landscape and light begin to dominate the scene. As well, brushstrokes grow larger, yet become less violent and jagged, perhaps in reaction both to the greater tranquility of his immediate ambiance and to developments in the art of the 1960s.

Montauk I of 1969 is a good example of one of the stages of his later style. Though it is nearly abstract, remnants of his women lurk, with suggestions of mascara'ed eyes, lipsticked lips, and creamy limbs. As is often the case in de Kooning's work, tension reigns. There is conflict between a rectilinear structure and jerky, curved lines; between milky and fleshy tones and garish, commercial colors.

ROMARE BEARDEN

b. Charlotte, North Carolina, 1914

SHE-BA

1970
Collage of paper, cloth, and
  synthetic polymer paint on
  composition board
122 x 91 cm. (48 x 35 7/8 in.)
The Ella Gallup Sumner and
  Mary Catlin Sumner Collection
Acquisition no. 1971.12

Among America's foremost black artists, Romare Bearden often incorporates themes of his heritage into his art. Born in North Carolina and raised in Harlem, Bearden has made the black experience one of his main motifs. Though there have been periods in his career when his art approached abstraction, he generally works representationally, a mode best suited to the chronicling of his culture. Bearden, however, never becomes overly anecdotal or illustrational, and his work invariably asserts convincing structural power.

SHE-BA is a collage done in 1970, and indeed, mixed materials have been Bearden's primary medium since 1963. Collage intrigued Bearden because it allowed him to thrust disparate but related events and moments into his work, and it best expressed his belief both in the kaleidoscopic variety of life and in the interconnectedness of past and present, of memory and being, and of different cultures. Moreover, collage permitted a textural and coloristic variety and richness that Bearden associated with the black world, especially with the great kingdoms of ancient Africa.

In this respect, the model for the woman in SHE-BA seems to be a fusion of a contemporary black woman and the famous Queen of Sheba. Her dress is more present-day, though eternally folkloric, and her placement in profile on a throne holding a scepter of sorts suggests her regality. Just as Bearden conflates past and present in the figure of She-ba, he blends a variety of styles in the work. The simplifications and stylizations of its form imply a variety of traditions including African, folk, and aspects of modern art, and the side view of the figure suggests Egyptian and other Near Eastern sources. Flat and decorative, with brightly patterned forms locked into a tight rectangular structure, SHE-BA reflects some of the most vital traditions in modern art, particularly the work of Matisse and Mondrian. Moreover, the use of collage evokes the material opulence of the ancient southern Arabian land of Sheba, a culture of great wealth, whose famous queen exchanged sumptuous gifts with King Solomon. In an assertion of black pride, Bearden most likely sees the country of Sheba, whose population also settled Ethiopia, as one of the great civilizations of the past.

SOL LEWITT

b. Hartford, Connecticut, 1928

***A WALL IS DIVIDED INTO
THREE EQUAL, NEARLY
SQUARE AREAS.
ONE IS PAINTED RED, ONE
YELLOW, ONE BLUE.
ON THE RED AREA,
VERTICAL LINES AND IN
THE CENTER OF THE AREA,
A SQUARE IS DRAWN,
WITHIN WHICH ARE
HORIZONTAL LINES.
ON THE YELLOW AREA,
VERTICAL LINES, AND IN
THE CENTER OF THE AREA,
A CIRCLE IS DRAWN,
WITHIN WHICH ARE
HORIZONTAL LINES.
ON THE BLUE AREA,
VERTICAL LINES, AND IN
THE CENTER, A TRIANGLE
IS DRAWN, WITHIN WHICH
ARE HORIZONTAL LINES.
ALL LINES ARE WHITE
CHALK 1½" APART.
THE VERTICAL LINES DO
NOT ENTER THE
GEOMETRIC FIGURES.***

1981
Paint and chalk on wall
314 x 1587.5 cm. (3 ft. 15 in. x
    17 ft. 13 in.)
Drawn by Jo Watanabe and David
    and Marianne Gunther
The Ella Gallup Sumner and Mary
    Catlin Sumner Collection
Acquisition no. 1981.4a–c

206

In Conceptual Art, an intriguing contemporary development, the artist assigns more importance to the idea behind the work than to the work itself. While this philosophy has become popular recently, its most eloquent origins lie in the art and writing formulated by Marcel Duchamp as early as the 1910s. Duchamp believed that all art begins with an idea, and since the transference of this idea into a conventional visual work of art tends to "muddy" the thought, the intelligent artist should keep his notion pure by dispensing with an intermediary object and allowing the idea to function as the work itself. In addition, Conceptualism satisfied the avant-garde demand both for increasingly novel and provocative works of art and for expanding the limits of the definition of art.

Sol LeWitt considers himself a Conceptual artist because almost invariably his works begin as a set of instructions that are carried out by assistants (like a composer whose music is performed by others). In this respect, his art is reminiscent of that produced in the Renaissance workshop, where the master artist laid down the basic designs and his studio completed the work. Although LeWitt's instructions often sound dull and dry, his finished products, as revealed in this wall piece for the Wadsworth Atheneum, are remarkably compelling. In typical fashion, LeWitt's work is done directly on the wall, and because this particular piece is located in a somewhat unusual space, it is impossible (as this photograph suggests) to take in all the work from any one vantage point. The painting is in the Morgan wing of the museum, on a wall that is two stories high. A balcony divides the room horizontally but stands clear of the wall. The painting is set into this architectural space and interacts with it. We view it here from the balcony, and only the upper portion is visible. From beneath the balcony, the viewer may see a fragment of the lower portion. This wall painting thus demands movement on the part of the spectator, and it compels the viewer to acknowledge the surrounding architecture and light. Although this geometric work, with its red, yellow, and blue ground overlaid with white chalk might recall some of Frank Stella's art of the early and mid-1960s, LeWitt's piece is unique in that the artist has been given his own wall in the museum to create something specifically for that environment. However, the history of wall drawings is a venerable tradition, and LeWitt's work might be seen as the most recent development of a tendency going back to the cave paintings of Altamira and Lascaux.

Index of Artists